PAST DEADLINES, PAST LIVES

PAST DEADLINES, PAST LIVES

NEWS, VIEWS AND SECOND THOUGHTS

Compiled by Garret Mathews
Introduction by Garret Mathews
Foreword by P.S. Wall

ALBION PRESS
Tampa, Florida

Copyright © 2001 by Garret Mathews

All rights reserved. No part of this publication may be reproduced or transmitted in any form or by any means, electronic or mechanical, including photocopying, recording, or any information storage and retrieval system, without permission in writing from the publisher.

05 04 03 02 01   1 2 3 4 5

Library of Congress Cataloging-in-Publication Data

Past deadlines, past lives : news, views and second thoughts / [compiled] by Garret Mathews
    p. cm.
  ISBN 0-9709170-5-8
    1. Journalists—United States—Biography. I. Mathews, Garret.

PN4781 .P37 2001
070'.92'273—dc21
[B]
                                                                                                                    2001022711

Jacket design: Antler Design Works
Design and typesetting: Sue Knopf/Graffolio

Published by Albion Press, Inc., Tampa, Florida.

Printed and bound in the United States of America.

To everybody who worked the night shift at the Bluefield Daily Telegraph in 1972. God, I miss it.

Contents

Foreword, P. S. Wall ix

Introduction, Garret Mathews x

Art Linkletter, television personality 3

Christiane Amanpour, CNN 4

Jill Lawrence, *USA Today* 5

Matthew Storin, *Boston Globe* 6

Walter Mears, Associated Press 7

Mort Walker, nationally syndicated cartoonist 8

Bob Verdi, *Golf Digest* 10

John Dancy, NBC News 11

Mark Boyle, Indianapolis Pacers 12

Alexander Wolff, *Sports Illustrated* 13

John McCaslin, *Washington (D.C.) Times* 14

Pat Hughes, WGN Chicago 16

Rheta Grimsley Johnson, *Atlanta Constitution* & King Features Syndicate 17

Jim Litke, The Associated Press 18

Dan Roan, WGN-TV Chicago 20

Tom Becka, KFAB Omaha 21

Bill Tammeus, *Kansas City Star* 22

David Halberstam, Miami Heat 24

Tom Cushman, *San Diego Union-Tribune* 25

Murray Olderman, *Palm Springs (California) Life* 26

Charlie Vincent, *Detroit Free Press* 28

Joe Tait, Cleveland Cavaliers 31

Stu Bykofsky, *Philadelphia Daily News* . . 32

Kenny Mayne, ESPN 35

Doug Robarchek, *Charlotte (North Carolina) Observer* 36

George Vecsey, *The New York Times* 38

Gordon Forbes, *USA Today* 42

Ernie Johnson, Milwaukee Braves 43

Hal McCoy, *Dayton Daily News* 44

B. Peter Carry, *Sports Illustrated* 46

Bruce Morton, CNN 48

David Shaw, *Los Angeles Times* 49

Art Thiel, *Seattle Post-Intelligencer* 50

Gil Stratton, CBS 51

Roger Simon, *U.S. News & World Report* 52

Kevin Harlan, CBS Sports, Turner Sports 54

Juan Williams, *Washington Post* 55

Jack Perkins, Arts & Entertainment Network 56

Marc Zumoff, Philadelphia '76ers 58

Betty Winston Bayé,
    Louisville Courier-Journal 59

Elaine Viets, nationally syndicated
    columnist 60

George Lardner, *Washington Post* 63

Georgie Anne Geyer, nationally
    syndicated columnist 64

Phil Mushnick,
    New York Post, TV Guide. 66

Kathleen Parker, nationally syndicated
    columnist 67

Ken Bode, Medill School of Journalism,
    Northwestern University 70

Mort Olshan, *Gold Sheet* 71

Richard Reeves, nationally syndicated
    columnist 72

John Carman, *San Francisco Chronicle* . . . 73

Rita Braver, CBS News 74

Mike Siegel, nationally syndicated talk
    show host 75

Michael Knisley, *Sporting News* 76

Josh Lewin, Fox TV 77

Sam Lowe, *Arizona Republic* 78

Marvin Kalb, Joan Shorenstein
    Center on the Press, Politics
    and Public Policy 80

George Herman, CBS News 83

P. S. Wall, Universal Press Syndicate 84

Jay Schadler, Bravo Network 86

Ron Fimrite, *Sports Illustrated* 87

Bil Keane, nationally syndicated
    cartoonist 88

Jonathan Alter, *Newsweek*, NBC News . . 90

Betty Beale, *Washington Post,
    Washington Star* 91

Ben Beagle, *Roanoke (Virginia) Times* . . . 94

Tom Tiede, nationally syndicated
    correspondent. 96

Bob Hill, *Louisville Courier-Journal* 98

Paul Harris, KTRS St. Louis 100

Jim Berry, nationally syndicated
    cartoonist 102

Steve Levy, ESPN. 104

Rob Hiaasen, *Baltimore Sun* 107

Barbara Naness, nationally syndicated
    columnist 106

Walt Brasch, professor of journalism . . 107

Foreword
by P. S. Wall

Journalism is not a career—it's a calling. You take the vow: poverty, servitude, and no time off for good behavior. My first editor also expected me to be chaste. I told him celibates don't work on Sundays, so he backed off.

On bad days you ask yourself, "What on Earth have I done with my life?" Newsprint is just one step up from writing on sand. Monday morning, your story is up for a Pulitzer. Tuesday, it's lining the birdcage. And television and radio stories dissipate into the air like steam.

But on the good days, when the story spills onto the page, or from the screen or the radio, and it's so good you're not sure where the words came from—there is no drug that can take you higher. And so, like Sisyphus, you sit your butt back at the keyboard and start pushing that baby up the hill again.

This book is about people in the media, and the sins we committed to get there. Mort Walker wins the lowest starting salary with $17.50 a week. John Carman's decision "to be, or not to be" a journalist began with the story of Pancho Villa's skull. And Roger Simon's early obits will kill you.

For journalists like Garret Mathews, becoming a reporter was his Holy Grail. For the rest of us, Kathleen Parker summed it up by saying, "My first newspaper job was a fluke, and my career, most likely a mistake."

People in media don't build the building. We make it safer. We don't run the city. We make the men and women who do, honest. We make the reader think. We make the reader feel.

And, sometimes, if we're very, very lucky, we make a difference.

P. S. Wall's internationally syndicated column, "Off the Wall," appears in ten million homes each week. The former newspaperwoman has written two top-selling books, *My Love Is Free . . . But the Rest of Me Don't Come Cheap* and *If I Were A Man, I'd Marry Me*.

Introduction
by Garret Mathews

Garret Mathews is a metro columnist on the *Evansville (Indiana) Courier & Press*. His first job in the media was at the *Bluefield (West Virginia) Daily Telegraph* in 1972.

The lede on my newspaper career was written on February 8, 1972.

That morning, I packed my worldly possessions into my Pinto and took off down the road. Because I wasn't very worldly, I only needed half the trunk.

Stereo, speakers, crate of records, Frisbee, pen-and-pencil set, W-2 form, three changes of clothes, scribbled directions that showed the way to the boarding house where I would share the bathroom with the eightysomething lady of the manor.

Such a piddling load. Why bother the movers?

I was scared to death.

The job was that of deskman. Never done it before.

I knew from the job interview that the grizzled men in the newsroom of the *Bluefield (West Virginia) Daily Telegraph* called each other "ace" and "stud" and drank beer until 6 o'clock in the morning. Never been around people like that.

Everybody knew how to "gimme six grafs," "bang out that agate," and "move your ass with that cutline." I didn't have a clue.

There was one other thing.

Impending financial ruin. The pay was $90 a week.

My father, who wanted me to work at the bank, sat me down with a sheet of paper the night before I was to leave.

"Still want that alternative lifestyle? A job where you don't have to sell somebody something?"

I nodded. That much I knew.

"Very well. On this side of the page, write down the sum of money you're going to make per month at the greasy newspaper."

He circled the meager amount.

"Now write your projected expenses."

College loan payment. Car payment. Food. Gasoline. Lodging. Underwear.

This total was time and a half more.

Dad circled it so forcefully the paper ripped.

I took off anyhow. Maybe the repo man wouldn't think to look for me in a boardinghouse.

My hometown radio station was the last link to the known world. I kept the dial where it was until the tunes had been completely overrun by a strange-sounding man reading death notices.

I hoped the voice wasn't being prophetic.

The elderly woman at the boardinghouse said we'd get along just fine. There were just a few rules to follow.

I could not do anything inside the dwelling that could even remotely be construed as noise.

I could not bring women up to my room.

She reached deep into her housecoat and pulled out a Bible.

"Morals in this country are going to the devil," she said, fanning herself with a church bulletin. "If I can keep just one boy from going bad . . ."

I wanted to go bad in the worst way, but living on $90 a week was as much as giving me a Good Conduct Medal.

I could not use the telephone longer than sixty seconds. An egg timer was beside the receiver.

I could only use one towel per day.

"This is a place of residence, not a laundry."

I looked around the room. Bed, desk, mirror, cabinet, trash can, Book of Psalms, closet, decorative urn, two washcloths carefully folded to look like praying hands—what more could someone starting his career below the poverty line ask for?

The Vienna sausages were starting to work on me, so I went into the bathroom, took a load off and contemplated my future.

Suddenly the woman burst into the room.

I tried to cover up, but my shirt was too short.

"Where you from anyway?" she said casually, while trying to get rid of a holding tank's worth of mucus. "You never said."

"I hated to complain on my first day of work, but there was no chair."

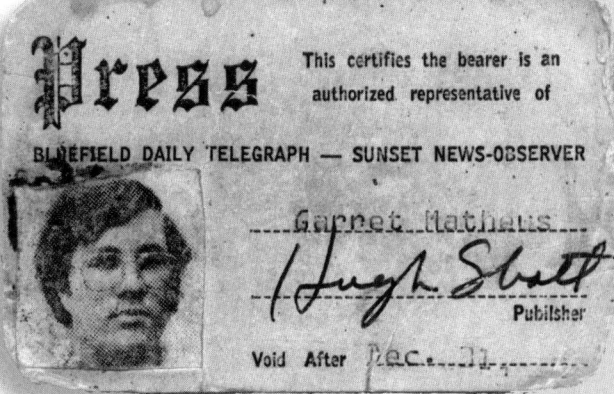

> "My hometown radio station was the last link to the known world. I kept the dial where it was until the tunes had been completely overrun by a strange-sounding man reading death notices."

"Abingdon, in southwest Virginia," I stammered, turning red in the face and no longer able to do what I had come in the bathroom to do.

"Two hours away."

I nodded. *When is she going to leave?*

"Do you know Bob and Jane Pullum? They're from down that way."

I shook my head.

She brought up another name. And another.

Desperately, I began making grunting and straining noises.

She looked at her watch.

"Got to go make supper. Don't forget to wash your hands."

I had just enough time to shower before going to the office and being with people who knew ten times more than me. The knobs looked like they were put in during Prohibition, so I didn't expect much. But to my surprise, both hot and cold water came out, more or less in a stream.

I lathered up and happened to look at my feet. They were bright red.

There was no pain, so it couldn't be blood. I leaned over and saw what looked like Ragu Sauce coming up the drain. Mounds of it.

I used up my one-towel allotment trying to get the red out of my ankles. The rest of the dry-off was with an undershirt.

"You've got to do something about the bathtub," I said, storming into the kitchen. "I'm nastier than I was when I went in."

"Oh, it's those darn pipes again."

She explained how the plumbing in the sink is connected to the works in the toilet. When gunk goes down the one, she said, it sometimes comes up the other.

"My legs look like dinner," I shouted. First being stupid and now discolored.

She promised to have it fixed when I got back. If not, I would receive two towels.

When I got to the newspaper building, I was too frightened to get out of the car. I leaned back in the seat and tried to force myself to sleep. The idea was that I'd wake up a twenty-year veteran of *The New York Times,* so good at my craft that I have scores of underlings to gimme my grafs.

In the years to come, I would dummy in the picture of the mangled

Gremlin for the front page the night our sports editor was killed in a car crash.

I would work with a police reporter who carried a gun to the office and moonlighted as a narc.

I would run naked down College Avenue at three o'clock in the morning with the head of the letterflex department.

I would assign our novice photographer to a high school football game and get less, or more, than I bargained for, depending on how you looked at it. He didn't think he had the skill to get a live-action shot, so he talked a member of each team into posing on the 50-yard-line before the game. He turned in a perfectly-crafted picture of a linebacker smearing a halfback. Two things gave it away. The ballcarrier was laughing. And he wasn't wearing a helmet.

I would be invited to watch an embalming. The mortician's regular help didn't show up, so I ended up passing the instruments.

I would work with a guy who routinely sneaked down to the pressroom to steal from lunch boxes. When he was found out, he tried to get rid of the evidence—and us—by setting the building on fire. It didn't come to much. The gothic structure had withstood eighty years of storms, pigeons, angry readers and poor reporters. It could handle a pint of lighter fluid, a match and a stack of Sunday newspapers.

I would work with an elderly sports columnist who referred to the local high school's ball teams as "Our Lads." He was a wrestling promoter on the side.

During the gasoline shortage of 1974, I would interview the mayor of a coalfield community who—when advised the only two stations in town were down to the fumes—hijacked a tanker truck.

During the flood of 1977, I would drive a Rescue Squad truck to the hospital while the EMT was in the back delivering a baby.

I would write several stories about a snake-handling church in southern West Virginia, and be on first-name basis with some of the members, including one disabled coal miner who has been bitten more than a hundred times by poisonous snakes. The last time I saw him, his hand had swollen

"When I got to the newspaper building, I was too frightened to get out of the car. I leaned back in the seat and tried to force myself to sleep."

> "During the flood of 1977, I would drive a Rescue Squad truck to the hospital while the EMT was in the back delivering a baby."

until it looked like a pus-covered basketball.

But this afternoon they had to send somebody down to get me.

"You the new guy?" one of the men from the newsroom said, peering in the car window.

"Uh, I guess so."

"Can't put the paper out down here, son. Let's go upstairs."

He looked up.

"Better park your car somewhere else."

I couldn't understand why. There was no telltale yellow marking on the curb. Must be a city ordinance, I wondered aloud.

"City doesn't care one way or the other, but your hood might," he said. "Get a little wind like we got today, and bricks start flying off the top of the building. Usually land about here. Almost killed this one guy. Put the story on page one."

I did what he said. I was already hopelessly behind. A blow to the head and I'd never catch up.

He led the way into the newsroom. My first impression was that a natural disaster had occcured within the walls and crews had been called in to assess the damage.

People were shouting into telephones and pounding manual typewriters that looked like they had seen duty against the Axis Powers. The AP teletype machines were ringing and practically jumping off the floor.

The floor was covered with paper, coffee cups, cigarette butts, overcoats, bank calendars from the 1960s, Smokey the Bear posters from the 1950s, lunch pails, hamburger wrappers, the remains of two no-longer-swiveling chairs and an area cordoned off by linked paperclips where several long fluorescent lightbulbs had crashed to the concrete floor.

"Somebody could cut the hell out of himself," my guide said, looking down. "Don't have any police tape, so that'll have to do until the janitors get their head out of their ass. Probably sometime next year."

He showed me the Depression-era bathroom with the swinging doors and the hole in the ceiling.

"Smells like raw sewage," I offered.

"Treated sewage," he said. "They put these big blue tablets in the commodes.

Look at it this way. The fixtures were installed during the Depression. You're shitting in a shrine."

He showed me the heavy-metal copy spike and said I should never play with it, that the last reporter to do so almost impaled himself. He warned me to be careful when eating at my desk because a week earlier peeling pieces of ceiling fell into the city editor's pizza and he almost bit into something that wasn't an anchovy.

I noticed jars on the table that looked to be full of congealed mayonnaise.

"Paste pots. You brush the stuff on to glue your copy paper together if you turn in more than one sheet."

He grinned.

"It's also pretty handy for grossing out the female employees."

He carefully affixed two globs under his nostrils until it looked like he had the mother of runny noses. Whistling and with his hand over his face, he sauntered out to composing and stopped next to a woman who was cutting down the next day's Dear Abby.

He pretended to sneeze.

"Bless you," she said.

"Thank you, my dear," he replied, casually lowering his hand to reveal his phony nasal condition.

The woman shrieked and left the room.

"Funnier than half the stuff you see on *Ed Sullivan*," he roared as he removed the evidence.

We walked downstairs to the break room. The television set, which only picked up one channel, had more chains draped around it than an axe murderer would wear at his preliminary hearing.

Nonetheless, he said there still was a plot afoot to steal it.

"Helps keep the wits sharp."

We took the gateless and, no doubt, inspectionless freight elevator up to the mailroom.

"Uh, er, I smell marijuana," I said as we stepped off.

"Sure you do. The insert stuffers get high as hell. About every other week, a cop comes in the newsroom with a warrant for one of them. We cover for the guy. Say he's been transferred."

I noticed tiny pot plants pushing up in the dirt floor.

"Circulation director lets 'em grow it.

> "He led the way into the newsroom. My first impression was that a natural disaster had occcured within the walls and crews had been called in to assess the damage."

xv

"We walked downstairs to the break room. The television set, which only picked up one channel, had more chains draped around it than an axe murderer would wear at his preliminary hearing."

Says it makes 'em work better."

He looked at the pile of mailbags.

"Free piece of advice for you, pal. Don't be up here when the newspapers come out. They'll think you're a new hire and they'll give you the initiation rite."

Which is?

"Stuff you in one of these mail sacks and throw you down the sixty-foot chute to the basement where the route men line up. If you don't holler loud enough, you'll be thrown in the back of somebody's station wagon and be part of the first edition to Bramwell."

We went back downstairs and he introduced me to my desk and a stack of copy paper beside the typewriter.

"Put heads on 'em," the city editor said.

I hated to complain on my first day of work, but there was no chair.

"There's three for every five employees. Either steal one, or learn to squat."

Fifteen minutes passed as I painfully composed "AME Church Choir To Meet" and "Bluewell Sewer Grant Approved."

The city editor looked over my shoulder.

"Gotta pick up the tempo, stud. We're not a monthly."

Nine hours later, the presses started. You could tell because it suddenly felt like the building had been hit by a train.

The grizzled men took me down to watch.

"You're on your way now, ace," one said as he pulled a newspaper off the conveyor belt.

I still have that newspaper. Nixon was getting ready to go to China, and the aircraft carrier *Kitty Hawk* was steaming toward Vietnam.

And on page nine, there's the headline on the sewer grant.

Written by a guy who finally came in from the car.

PAST DEADLINES, PAST LIVES

I contacted prominent men and women who work in print, TV, and radio and asked them to tell me a story about when they were just starting out in the business.

It can be about the primitive working conditions, I said, or the lack of pay that you believed to be life-threatening, or you can look back on one or more of the eccentric characters you left behind. It's up to you.

Garret Mathews

Here's what they had to say . . .

... no idea ... I would be broadcasting on all three networks ...

It was a warm June day in 1933. The nation was in the depths of the worst depression in history. I was in the kitchen of the college cafeteria making Waldorf salad, one of three jobs I had while working my way toward a teaching degree with a major in English at San Diego State College. The telephone rang for me, and over the clatter of the kitchen crew I heard a stranger say, "My name is Lincoln Deller. I am the manager of the CBS station KGB in San Diego, and I heard you win a debate on the campus last month, and since then I've learned you also write a humor column and that you've just written a musical comedy for this year's Aztec Follies. I am just wondering if you would be interested in a job as a radio announcer."

I quickly said yes, although I had never dreamed of being in show business. I did not ask about the hours, the salary, the retirement pay, vacations, stock options or any other topic concerning my possible employment. Remember, this was 1933. The following week I was doing announcements and reading commercials nightly from 1 P.M. to 1 A.M. and getting $75 a month. I had no idea that in the next few years I would be broadcasting my own shows on all three networks on a nationwide basis, and that six decades later I would be on the air with Bill Cosby on CBS on Friday nights at 8 P.M. with *Kids Say the Darndest Things*.

Art Linkletter is a longtime television personality.

Linkletter (kneeling at left) at America's Exposition, San Diego, California, 1935.

... I arrived at CNN in Atlanta ... with $115, a bicycle, and a suitcase

Christiane Amanpour is chief international correspondent for CNN.

In September of 1983, I arrived at CNN headquarters in Atlanta with $115, a bicycle and a suitcase. I felt rather lucky since these were the cheap and cheerful early days of Cable News Network, and I had just been hired on the basis of a telephone interview in which I was asked, among other things, what's the capital of Iran? Since I am Iranian, I got the answer right, and from day one I felt rather good about my future with this network.

There were several cultural clashes, as you can imagine …

My first job in journalism was at UPI in Charleston, West Virginia, in 1977. It was a bureau in transition. The company had just sent in an ambitious, hard-driving bureau chief from outside the state. The staff was an odd combination of oldtimers who were West Virginia natives and two young Jewish women who had lived within blocks of each other in Greenwich Village, but only met each other when UPI sent both to West Virginia.

There were several cultural clashes, as you might imagine. The one I remember best was this: Anita Bryant was in the throes of her campaign against homosexuality and I had gone to Marshall University in Huntington, West Virginia, to cover one of her rallies. I wrote a story for the next day's morning papers. Then, as was the custom, I rewrote it for afternoon newspapers the next day.

The stories for afternoon papers started running on the wire at midnight in the PMs report. The editor responsible for the copy in that cycle was an old hand from Beckley, West Virginia. I was the morning person. When I arrived around 5:45 A.M. and read what was on the wire under my byline, I nearly went into shock.

Every time I had used the word "homosexual" in the Anita Bryant story, it had been changed to "pervert." Within seconds I was on the phone to my bureau chief in an apoplectic state. He had a hard time believing me, and I still have a hard time believing it really happened. I fixed the copy in short order, but the memory lives on.

Jill Lawrence is a political writer at *USA Today*. Formerly a columnist for The Associated Press, she has covered every presidential campaign since 1988.

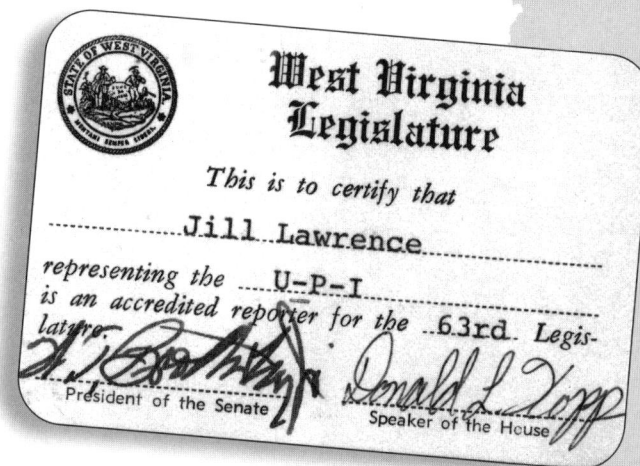

... I came within millimeters of ending my newspaper career ...

Matthew Storin is editor of the *Boston Globe*.

My first day in the newspaper business was in 1962 when I was a summer intern at the *Springfield (Massachusetts) Daily News*. I was assigned to one of those huge desks we had in those days with a typewriter bolted to a well that could be closed so there was a flat surface on top.

When the typewriter was in use, the desk afforded a fair amount of work space on the right side, but just three inches of room to the left of the well. At mid-morning (this was an afternoon paper), there was a coffee break. I joined my colleagues as they went downstairs and bought an orange soda. I returned to my desk and set the bottle down on that three inches of space between the typewriter well and the edge of the desk.

Then the city editor yelled out, "Storin, take an obit." I put the phone to my ear and started to type away. I was perhaps three quarters of the way across the first line when I realized that if I typed one more syllable, I was going to knock over the bottle with the typewriter carriage, sending the contents all over the papers of the gruff-looking reporter next to me. A bundle of nerves that day, I was convinced that I came within millimeters of ending my newspaper career in the first three hours.

The guy sitting next to me turned out to be a nice fellow. But it was such a traumatic moment I've never forgotten it.

I had to open a new AP bureau ...

I first worked for The Associated Press in a temp job in Boston in 1955. I returned there after graduating from college in 1956 and then was transferred to Montpelier, Vermont, in December of that year as the first AP correspondent there.

I was twenty-one at the time. The pay was all the way up to $60 a week. I had to open a new AP bureau, winging it since there is no instruction book on how to start one. The bureau was a desk in the attic of the Vermont Statehouse (it was called the Crow's Nest) which served as a press room for a consortium of Vermont newspapers. (Two AMs dominated, and six PMs shared the product a cycle late.) Basically, my assignment was to serve the PM newspapers.

I set out from Boston in my aging Chevy and ran into a snowstorm before I got to the Vermont line. It took me most of the night to plow my way in. I found a cheap hotel room (they were all cheap in those days) and went to work, carrying my portable typewriter, which was my only equipment.

The itinerant AP fix-it technician had preceded me, so there was a teletype and a tape-punching keyboard already installed. All I had to do was turn it on. And figure out how to make it work, because I had never used one before.

Somehow, it all came together, with no small help from my new colleagues, including the *Burlington Free Press* guy, who showed me which desk was mine.

A few days later, the legislature arrived. Never covered one of those, either. But I watched the veterans, listened to the pols and figured out that, covering legislature and politics, if you could ask a sensible question and accurately write down the answer, you'd probably be OK.

It was training by total immersion on the job. I guess it worked. I never had more fun as a newsman.

Walter Mears of The Associated Press won a Pulitzer Prize in 1977 for political reporting on the 1976 presidential campaign. He has been Washington bureau chief for the AP and served a stint as executive editor.

They asked me, "How do you like our cards?" "They stink."

Mort Walker draws the nationally syndicated comic strip "Beetle Bailey."

We were poor and I had so many jobs during my youth—delivering newspapers, selling magazines, doing yardwork, caddying, delivering for the drug store—that my first *real* job was fantastic. I was trying to put myself through Kansas City Junior College by working part-time at night in the shipping department of Hallmark Cards. I answered a blind ad for an artist, and it turned out to be for Hallmark in the editorial department upstairs. It was 1942 and the war had just started. Women had always bought most of the cards, but Hallmark sensed a new market emerging with soldiers needing to send greetings.

They asked me, "How do you like our cards?" I was seventeen and hadn't yet learned the art of diplomacy.

"They stink," I replied.

They reeled and asked, "Why?"

I explained that their cards were too sickly sweet for any man to send. They looked at my humorous card samples and hired me on the spot at $17.50 a week. Up to that point, you seldom saw humorous greeting cards. I feel I started a whole new trend. Almost all the cards today are humorous.

TAKE IT EASY, SOLDIER

DON'T LET <u>NOTHIN'</u> GET YOU DOWN!

Walker's first comic strip, "The Limejuicers," ran for a year in 1936 in the *Kansas City Journal*. He was 13.

... going after that ghoul was better training than I thought.

Bob Verdi writes for *Golf Digest* magazine. A longtime sportswriter on The *Chicago Tribune*, he still contributes one column a week.

My first newspaper job was on the *Long Island (New York) Press*, which has since folded.

I wanted to cover baseball and basketball, but I was put on the overnight desk. One of my first assignments was to write about a ghoul at this cemetery who was going around tipping over gravestones looking for remains.

I remember creeping around with the police thinking, *What about baseball?*

I wasn't around at the time, but they finally ended up catching the guy.

I later wrote about the Chicago Cubs. As it turned out, going after that ghoul was better training than I thought.

... I flipped the page to what I expected to be the noon Dow ...

I was hired at KYW-TV in Cleveland to anchor a new half-hour program called the *Noon News*. It was 1961, and thirty-minute news programs were still a new idea. We were still learning how to do "long-form" news.

We—the production staff and I—realized the Dow Jones noon stock averages came over the AP wire machine at about ten minutes past noon every day. We decided we could include them in the show by having a writer rip them from the machine, bring them to the studio, and put them in the proper place in the script. The TelePrompTer was a new-fangled invention, and too expensive and complicated for a local news operation, so the anchors read from a sheaf of papers they held in their hands.

One day, not long after we had gone on the air, I was reading the news, and flipped the page to what I expected to be the noon Dow, ad-libbing as I did, "And now, the noon Dow Jones averages . . ."

To my horror, I discovered there was no page with the averages on it. In a flash, I decided to, well, extemporize.

"Industrials are up point-oh-three, transportations down point-oh-five, and utlities down point-oh-one." (I was smart enough not to have the market making a major move.)

When I got back to the newsroom after the broadcast, the news director asked me where I got those stock averages.

Trapped, I admitted that I had made them up.

"I thought so," he said. "It's Memorial Day. The market is closed."

John Dancy was a senior correspondent at NBC News, where he worked for 31 years.

If you think talking about ice melting for an hour nonstop is easy ...

Mark Boyle does radio play-by-play for the Indianapolis Pacers in the NBA.

I landed my first job in the spring of 1978 in Miles City, Montana, a town of about ten thousand in the eastern part of the state. Although I aspired to be a play-by-play broadcaster, I was asked to do everything from reading the farm reports to running a classical music disc jockey shift. I made $500 a month, plus a talent fee of $10 for every game I broadcast. I vividly remember looking forward to high school basketball tournaments, not so much because I enjoyed the work (although I did), but because we would do four games in a day and I would enhance my anemic bank account by $40, meaning that it was possible I might be able to eat that week.

I lived in an apartment at the top of a treacherous hill on the banks of the Yellowstone River. The rent was $90 a month, which was about all I could afford at the time. The reason it was so cheap was that in the winter the hill would ice up, making it an even bet that you would wind up in the river if you weren't extraordinarily careful on the downhill drive.

The river would freeze every winter, which meant it would thaw again every spring with potential for flooding.

Since I lived in a place that provided a clear shot of the river, the station would send me home with remote broadcast gear and ask me to do a live play-by-play of the ice breakup. If you think talking about ice melting for an hour nonstop is easy, I suggest you try it some time. I hated it at the time, but now I must admit it was valuable experience. If I could handle that, it's not likely I'm going to come across anything in an NBA game I can't deal with.

"That's two takes right there."

In the late 1970s, I was a freshman at Princeton University, trying to learn the business and earn a little spending money by stringing campus news for the *Times* of Trenton, New Jersey, fifteen miles away. Being so close to the school, the *Times* would eagerly publish at least a few paragraphs on just about anything. That spring, the university decided to grant honorary degres to its usual brace of people, and I called the city desk to see what the paper would want off the graduation ceremony—how many "takes," or double-spaced, typewritten pages via telecopier.

The city editor was a hard-boiled, blunt-talking veteran with the irresistible name of Harry Blaze. He wanted to know who would be receiving honorary degrees. I told him one of the honorees would be a Russian cello virtuoso.

Harry heard me spit out the name "Mstislav Rostropovich" and said, "That's two takes *right there*."

Alexander Wolff is a senior writer at *Sports Illustrated* and has written a half-dozen books.

...my fits of hyperventilation ... almost got me fired

John McCaslin is a columnist on the *Washington (D.C.) Times*.

Class of 1980 diploma in hand, I came home to the Nation's Capital, anxious to give journalism a go, and maybe even write my way into the Watergate sequel.

What did I know?

"You need experience, sport," consoled my longtime friend and neighbor, Jeremiah O'Leary, White House correspondent for the old *Washington Star*. "A place where you can learn the ropes."

At age twenty-two, I had lived my entire life inside the Beltway. My mother, however, grew up in Montana, and every summer of my childhood we piled into the family station wagon—parents, three sons, panting dog—to visit my grandmother, Notie Larson.

There is no place on Earth more beautiful than Montana. So what better place, I now asked myself, to launch a career in journalism? Go West, young man!

In Montana, anyplace with more people than sheep is referred to as a city. Even if the city slogan is, "Where the hell is Kalispell?" Actually, it's the gateway to Glacier National Park and home to the state's finest ski resort, the Big Mountain. Of more interest to me, the valley supported one daily, four weeklies, more than a half-dozen radio stations, and one television station.

My first discovery that warm July day I pulled into town wasn't the Mount St. Helens ash that still coated everything a hose couldn't reach. It was the way I talked. Mark Holston, news director for KCFW-TV, broke the news.

"You have a Southern accent," he told me. Nobody else was hiring either.

For the next month, I sold ski boots at the Ski Haus. Never did it occur to customers, as I explained how a boot should fit for optimum downhill comfort performance, that I'd never strapped on a pair of skis in my life.

I moved into a one-room cabin next door to Grand Notie's gingerbread cottage at the foot of the Rocky Mountains. The cabin had no bathroom, so I visited my grandmother often. If the hour was late (Kalispell is home to many fine drinking establishments; my favorite was Moose's Saloon), a pine tree sufficed until morning.

Worried that the first autumn snowfall would blow my cover at the Ski Haus, I paid a visit to G. George

Ostrom, award-winning columnist for the *Hungry Horse News* and editor of the *Kalispell Weekly News*. A native of the Flathead Valley, George as a young married man was legislative aide to Senator Mike Mansfield. He wasn't shy in saying he couldn't wait to leave Washington.

George didn't judge a journalist by his accent, rather on his ability to write and, most importantly, sleep with a camera. George told me he had no openings, but he had heard that radio station KOFI (pronounced "coffee") was looking for a news director. An hour later, after listening to my unscheduled sales pitch, KOFI owner Bill Patterson agreed to give me a a two-week tryout. (I later learned he owed George a favor or two.)

Soon, every KOFI listener in the valley was asking Patterson about the kid from "down South," who surely wasn't schooled properly if he couldn't pronounce simple words like "Kokanee" salmon and "Salish-Kootenai" Indian. But it was my fits of hyperventilation that almost got me fired before I was hired.

I owe my career to Curt Shurgart, the station's most popular disc jockey and practical joker. Curt actually lived in a cabin smaller than mine, although his was equipped with an outhouse. As I gasped my way through another newscast during my first week on the job, Curt decided to make my life even worse by striking a match to the story I was reading. To his amazement, and certainly mine, not only did I manage to blow out the flames without injury, but did so between paragraphs, never missing a beat. From that newscast on, fainting on the air was the least of my concerns.

In September 1980, two months after I arrived in Kalispell, Patterson gave me the job—starting pay, $1,000 a month, on condition I buy my own gas. The experience was worth every nickel. A few days later, three people were mauled to death by grizzly bears in Glacier Park. Then the Amtrak Empire Builder derailed atop the Continental Divide at Marias Pass, injuring scores of passengers. Unlike Washington, D.C., where there is a scribe on every block, I was the only reporter in sight. As Jerry O'Leary promised, plenty of space to learn the ropes.

"'You have a Southern accent,' he told me.'"

I considered it a live broadcast, meaning I never had any do-overs.

Pat Hughes does radio play-by-play for the Chicago Cubs on WGN.

I started out in 1979 on KRVE in Los Gatos doing San Jose Bees' games in the California League. The pressbox consisted of a card table and a folding chair. I was the extent of the press corps, and it made me feel like I was someone special. They paid me $25 a game.

I talked into a microphone and a tape recorder. The games were on a tape-delay basis, meaning it might be twelve or more hours before they got on the air. Nobody was in a hurry, though. My commentary would be edited down and they'd insert the commercials.

There was no publicity stuff handed out. If you wanted material to talk about between pitches, you had to gather it yourself. I considered it a live broadcast, meaning I never had any do-overs. That would have been making things easy on myself, and I don't think that's a good way to learn to do it right.

... to eat we had swap-outs with our restaurant advertisers ...

I didn't have enough sense just to go to work for a newspaper straight out of journalism school. I tried to *start* one.

I had honeymooned on St. Simons Island, off the Georgia coast. My new husband and I looked around, saw no newspaper on this green Eden, and decided we'd soon fix that.

We arrived on that swell island with a Pinto pulling a U-Haul filled with some obsolete typesetting equipment and our utility-wire dining room table. Ten days later, we published the first issue of the *St. Simons Sun*.

Neither of us could sell ads. A few charitable businesses kept the paper afloat. We never had enough money to pay ourselves, so to eat we had swap-outs with our seafood restaurant advertisers. After the St. Simons experience, it was years before I could look at a shrimp again.

We hadn't counted on several things. The island was a retirement destination, with people from all over, which makes for a rather loose community. We begged for brides. We gave away classifieds and bikes. We printed local news nobody cared about.

The shoppers we had dismissed as "not real newspapers" and no competition were fat with ads. (They still exist today.) Our baby died after 26 weeks. the *Sun* officially set on Christmas Day, 1975, right after we threw free copies to three thousand homes. I still have a strong right arm.

Rheta Grimsley Johnson writes four columns a week for the *Atlanta Constitution* and King Features Syndicate. She is a past winner of the Ernie Pyle Award.

A day didn't pass without somebody threatening to blow up my car

Jim Litke has been national sports columnist for The Associated Press since 1989.

I played competitive soccer all the way through college and was the sports editor of my high school paper, so I thought I knew something about the passion our games elicit. But my first year in the newspaper business (1974) taught me otherwise.

Like most beginners in sports departments, I was assigned to cover preps. The beat was in and around New Haven, Connecticut. While the football season produced nothing memorable, that changed the moment I saw my first West Haven-Hamden hockey game. The two suburbs were like oil and water. West Haven was then a blue-collar, predominantly Catholic suburb. Hamden was a more affluent, predominantly Protestant area.

After the first game, a carload of kids from one high school ran a carload of cheerleaders from the other off the road. Before the second game, a kid leaned over the ice and tried to spray opposing players with ammonia. As luck would have it, Hamden and West Haven wound up playing for the state championship at Yale University's Ingalls Rink at the end of the season.

I wasn't a columnist then, but other than the score, there wasn't a mention of what happened in the game until the eighth paragraph. The first seven were taken up describing the ugliness surrounding the play—adults spitting on kids, obscene gestures from the players to the crowd, etc. And the post-game incidents were even worse. While the trophy was being presented, the West Haven coach pulled his team off the ice. While Hamden's captain, who was black, skated around the rink with the trophy held aloft, West Haven fans wearing KKK hoods could be seen in the crowd. Not surprisingly, when the Hamden captain skated past the West Haven bench, he defiantly thrust his middle finger in the air.

It was a sobering experience. A day didn't pass the following week without somebody calling me at home or work, threatening to blow up my car or my apartment or both. The following Sunday, the back page of the sports section was filled with letters from fans of both teams complaining that they had been unfairly portrayed. The last one published chastised both sides and advocated a one-year "cooling-off" period before any more games between them.

It was the only real comfort I took from the episode. But it taught me a lesson I've carried with me throughout my career: The way to keep perspective is to write what you see.

I was sure I was a dead man ...

Dan Roan is a sports reporter on WGN-TV in Chicago.

I went to work at WCIA-TV in Champaign, Illinois, right out of college in 1977. They made me the bureau chief in nearby Decatur. I was given an old CP-16 film camera complete with a huge body brace that had to be worn whenever the camera was used.

One day, I was standing on the edge of an overpass shooting down at a railyard fire about 250 feet below when a man in a passing car threw a string of firecrackers out his window toward me. With the weight of the camera and the brace, I was sure I was a dead man—if not from the fall, then from the gunshots I was certain were being aimed at me.

Fortunately, I caught myself before the fall, realized there was no gun, and took the rest of the day off to make my hair stop standing on end. At that time, beginning reporters at WCIA were making $160 a week. Beginning camerapersons made $150. They were paying me $140 a week—to do both jobs AND to live in Decatur. Many times I wondered if I had chosen the right line of work.

A drunk on the other end started to talk about committing suicide.

I remember my first Christmas at my first job. I was working as a disc jockey from midnight to 6 A.M. on KUGR in Green River, Wyoming, a town of about 13,000 people. It was cold outside, and I was miserable inside because I had to work such a lousy shift on a holiday.

About 2 A.M. the request line rang. A drunk on the other end started to talk about committing suicide. It seems that over the last year his daughter had died, and his wife had left him, and he saw no need to go on living. We talked for the next four hours. The main thing I wanted to do was just get him through the night. When my shift ended, he was feeling better and he thanked me for listening.

That Christmas morning, I realized that as a broadcaster you have a responsibility not only to your total audience but to your individual audience members as well. I don't know if he really would have committed suicide, but I was glad I could help.

Tom Becka is a talk show host on radio station KFAB in Omaha, Nebraska. He also is a stand-up comedian.

Irv … was too busy to ask for many details. "Get on it," he said.

Bill Tammeus of the *Kansas City Star* is a nationally syndicated editorial page columnist.

My ego is no bigger than that of most journalists. Which means it's about the size of Nevada. But early in my first job (1967-70) as a reporter at the now-defunct *Rochester (New York) Times-Union*, I noticed that stories I'd turn in early would get buried inside the paper. How could I gain any fame when my words were being used as a wall to keep the classified ads from crashing into the news hole?

Inside placement was especially true of enterprise stories from my beat, which had to do with subsidized housing, poverty, race relations and urban dynamics. If I handed in a lucid and erudite tome on moderate-income housing for the next afternoon's paper, the story would appear on page 5B along with birth notices and briefs about zoning board of appeals hearings on changes in category C-2 to C-3, whatever those were.

So one afternoon, as I worked on a stunning thumb-sucker about a relatively small change in an urban renewal plan, I decided to try a small and harmless experiment.

I hustled up to my assistant city editor. "Irv," I said, "I've just heard about some changes in urban renewal that could affect the whole city. I'm going to try to piece it together for tomorrow's paper."

Irv, as usual, was too busy to ask for many details. "Get on it," he said.

Get on it? I had been on it for a day and a half. The story was more than half-written. Only this time I hadn't begun to paste up the copy pages into a long strip. Instead, I kept it in separate takes and waited to unload it until much closer to deadline tomorrow— on the hunch the story would get better play.

One reason I suspected I could avoid getting buried on an inside page is that Irv and other assistant city editors made up most of the inside pages the day before with whatever they had on hand. Makeup of the front page of the Metro section and, of course, the front of the A section always waited until day of publication to keep the options open on breaking news.

I finished the urban renewal story before I left that afternoon and put it, separate page by separate page, in my drawer. In the morning, I told Irv I needed a little more information, but thought I could have the story by at least half an hour before deadline. I went on to other things. About twenty-five minutes before deadline, I ran up to Irv and said I could give him the urban renewal story, but it would come take by take.

"This is a good piece," I promised.

Five minutes later, I pulled the first take out of my drawer, scribbled "MORE" on the bottom and hollered for a copyperson to run it up to Irv. Ten minutes later, I sent up the second take. Then the third. Finally, a few minutes before deadline I ran the final few paragraphs up to the city desk myself. I acted excited. Almost breathless.

When the paper came out, there was my urban renewal story spread across the bottom of the front page of the Metro section. I smiled.

And for the next couple of years, whenever I had a story I suspected would get buried inside, I'd use the same ruse. The result was that for several years, housing and urban development stories seemed to become pretty important news in Rochester.

I never knew if Irv caught on. He was a wonderful man, but he died too young. Some day—assuming we both end up in the same warm eternal abode—I'm going to confess to him. He'll probably tell me he knew exactly what I was doing, agreed with me, and helped me pull it over on the city editor.

Assistant city editors are like that. You just can't trust 'em.

> "When the paper came out, there was my urban renewal story spread across the bottom of the front page of the Metro section. I smiled."

... my ability and willingness to sell has been ... indispensable

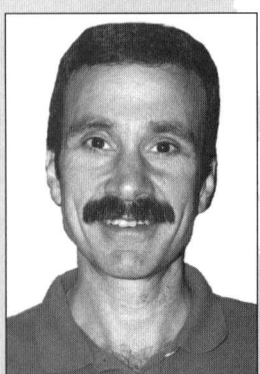

David Halberstam was the voice of St. John's University basketball team for fourteen years and spent six seasons as the radio voice of the Miami Heat in the NBA. He wrote *Sports on the New York Radio: A Play-By-Play History* about the history of radio sports.

When I wanted to put the St. John's basketball games on radio in the early 1970s, I was thrown out of a great many New York City radio stations. The Knicks couldn't get all their games on radio back then, so St. John's didn't have a prayer. When I finally did convince a surburban Long Island radio station to commit to the broadcasts, the station manager pulled the Yellow Pages out of his credenza and said, "Now sell it, young man."

For an aspiring play-by-play man, it was the beginning of a career that has now spanned almost thirty years of being on-air and selling advertising time off-air. Over the years, I was able to graduate from St. John's to the major New York City stations and later to the NBA. I never did shed the Yellow Pages or any other source for sales leads. Through the years, my ability and willingness to sell has been an indispensable complement to my on-air package, not to mention the meals the commissions put on my table.

When I started with St. John's, we sold $10,000 in spots the first season. When I left for the Miami Heat in 1992, we were billing well over $1 million a year. Coach Lou Carnesecca, Chris Mullin, the Big East and the St. John tradition had something to do with it, believe me.

... a young college golfer who had been attracting some attention ...

Two weeks after graduating from the University of Missouri School of Journalism, I arrived in Colorado Springs, Colorado, to begin dazzling readers of the *Gazette-Telegraph,* which had obtained my services for $65 a week (plus guaranteed overtime).

My start date coincided with the beginning of the U.S. Amateur Golf Tournament, which was to take place at the nearby Broadmoor Golf Club. As junior member of a three-man sports staff, my first assignment was to do a feature on a young college golfer who had been attracting some attention—mine not included. The only thing I knew about golf was that it involved a ball that I couldn't hit straight. Nevertheless, I reported to the Broadmoor as ordered and eventually located my subject, who was on the sixth hole of a practice round.

To fully comprehend the ensuing developments, one must understand the eccentricities of Rocky Mountain golf. The Broadmoor course was sprinkled along the eastern slope of Cheyenne Mountain, and its contours could prove deceptive to the unaware.

I'd soon learn the appropriate drill. Before putting, always look to see where you are in regard to the mountain. If it's directly behind you, what appears to be an uphill putt actually can be flat, or even downhill.

I didn't understand this on that first day, and neither did my golfer. When I saw him, he was leaning over a ten-foot putt, which he promptly rolled past the hole and off the green.

Returning to the clubhouse, I phoned the office and said to the sports editor, "Why should I write about this guy? He can't even play."

The editor's reply: "Write about him anyhow."

I did. That day, for several days afterward, and then for the next forty years. In an extraordinary thirty-six-hole final, he defeated amateur legend Charlie Coe, two up, to win the 1959 U.S. Amateur.

His name, which I had by then committed to memory, was Jack Nicklaus.

Tom Cushman is senior sports columnist on the *San Diego Union-Tribune.*

There ensued an interrogation about my sex life ...

Murray Olderman is a columnist and cartoonist whose work was distributed by Newspaper Enterprise Association to 750 daily newspapers. He retired from the syndicate in 1987. He is sports editor of *Palm Springs (California) Life* magazine.

A Rorschach test in downtown Chicago launched my fulltime career as a professional journalist in Sacramento, California. Anomalous as it might sound, that's the way it happened.

I was doing my graduate work in journalism at Northwestern University near Chicago when I consulted an *Editor & Publisher Yearbook* and sent out seventy letters to newspapers all over the country, seeking employment. I had one thing working for me. While mulling such abstracts as "Theories of Journalism," I also managed to get a few cartoons published in the sports section of the *Chicago Daily News*.

This was in the prehistoric days before Kinko's and copy machines. So I simply put the original drawings up on a wall of my Evanston, Illinois, apartment and photographed them with a Leica I had "liberated" for a couple of cartons of cigarettes in World War II Germany. In each of my query letters, I included three snapshots of my cartoons.

I actually got job offers from such diverse locales as Des Moines, Salt Lake City, and St. Louis, and there was an intriguing response from the *Sacramento Bee,* which appealed to my wife because her mother was living in California. That newspaper was interested in hiring me for the sports staff as a cartoonist-writer. But first, would I go down to the Loop in Chicago for an interview?

Sure. I took an elevated train to the office of a high-powered employment agency on Michigan Avenue. There ensued a fifteen-minute interrogation about my sex life and my attitude toward marriage. Not a word about my qualifications to be a journalist, or even a cartoonist. Then I was confronted with a series of ink blots and asked to interpret them. That was the Rorschach personality test.

A week later, I received a letter from the editor of the *Bee*. I was hired, sight unseen, at $65 a week—$25 more than they would have paid me in Des Moines. Right after graduation, we headed west by car, detoured north to South Dakota because of floods in Iowa, and then got stuck behind a cattle drive on a national highway in Wyoming that was still part dirt road and drove unannounced into downtown Sacramento.

The *Bee*, the bell cow of the well-regarded and successful McClatchy Newspapers that dated back to the days of the Gold Rush, was in its original building without air conditioning (the temperature exceeds one hundred degrees during the summer in Central California) and its walls were adorned by yellowing varnished full-page press mats of the newspaper's old issues.

The sports staff consisted of three grizzled writers who had been there a collective ninety years and were each old enough to be my father. All stories were processed through the central copy desk of the paper. Some of the editors didn't know a fumble from a miscue.

But I was lucky. I came under the wing of an old bullpen artist named Courtney Alderson and a brilliant editorial cartoonist, Newton Pratt, who taught me the nuances of drawing for publication—what paper to use, what kinds of pens and brushes and crayons—so that I actually perfected my techniques on the job. The old boys in sports left me completely alone to cover what I wanted. I did feature stories accompanied by cartoons. It was a great learning experience and prepared me for a lifetime in journalism.

Oh, yes. After about a month on the job, a guy in the personnel department of the paper confided in me that the report from the agency in Chicago, which had given me that ink blot test, had pronounced me a "good employment risk."

... a skinny 125-pound, six-footer with Buddy Holly glasses

Charlie Vincent retired from the *Detroit Free Press* in 1999. He was three times named among the top five columnists in the United States by The Associated Press Sports Editors.

I knew when I was a sophomore in high school—back in the long ago days when a man did not have to graduate from college to get into the journalism business and a woman could not get in at all—that I wanted to be a sportswriter.

In Victoria, Texas, I subscribed to the *Boston Globe* and the *Boston Post*, partially because I thought Ted Williams was the greatest baseball player who ever lived, but even more to read Hy Hurwitz and Clif Keane and Harold Kaese.

I never thought I'd interview Williams, never thought of covering a Major League baseball game, let alone a World Series, the Kentucky Derby, the NBA playoffs, the Masters, soccer's World Cup, or the Olympics.

When I was in high school, Major League baseball was played no farther west or south than St. Louis.

But I fell in love with words and with the deeds of athletes, and just before I graduated from St. Joseph's High School in May of 1958, I walked into the office of the weekly *Victoria Mirror* and asked for a job. The editor was a man named Grant Sorrell, who said his credentials included working for *Women's Wear Daily*. I do not know anything about *Women's Wear Daily*, but I knew I would have been more impressed if he had told me he had worked for the *Sporting News*.

The *Mirror* had been a family-owned operation for a long time, a mostly-ignored weekly in a growing town that had its own daily paper, the *Victoria Advocate*. At age eighteen, I didn't have much of an understanding of such things, but the *Advocate* was the voice of the establishment, the old money, the cattle ranchers, who also owned the oil wells and the banks and the land—the people whose ancestors had settled this part of coastal Texas one hundred or more years ago and grown rich in the process.

They built a little downtown around a city square with a couple of banks across from each other, a couple of movie theaters for English-speaking patrons and one for those who spoke Spanish, and for the first half of the twentieth century, Victoria orbited around those few square blocks.

But in 1958, an outsider bought up some land a few miles north of downtown, laid out plans for Victoria's first shopping center and, fearing that the entrenched aristocracy would torpedo his plans through the strength of their voice in the *Advocate*, bought the *Mirror* from the family who had owned it for so many years.

It was into that developing drama of small-town political and economic intrigue that I walked, a teenager who wanted nothing more than to write about what high school athletes accomplished on a Friday night on a dimly-lit football field.

"Well," Grant Sorrell told me, "we don't really need anybody to write sports. What we need is somebody to sell advertising, write a few stories a week, rewrite some press releases, answer phones and help clean the place up, sweep out, things like that. When you have time, you can cover some games if you want to, and we'll get them in the paper if we have space."

I jumped at the opportunity, even though it paid $25 a week at the time when the minimum wage was $1 an hour.

I did it for about a year. Eventually, they let me write a sports column every week. They had a photographer take my picture and used it with the column, just like they did in the Houston papers. Or in Boston.

I sold a little advertising, swept a lot of floors, rewrote a lot of press releases, and learned to take pictures. I was in journalism. And I was happy. I was living at home, going to Victoria Junior College at night, and probably should not have rocked the boat. But I did.

I figured a guy should get a raise once a year or so. Especially a guy making $25 a week. So in March of 1959 I made an appointment to see the owner of the newspaper. His office was not in the rundown little storefront that served as the newspaper's office, in a down-at-the-heels part of town, but in his newly constructed shopping center.

He was a pompous man, and he wore his gray hair long and flowing down the back of his neck. He called himself "The Colonel" and told people he had been given that honorary title somewhere back in time, before he arrived in Victoria.

I was a skinny 125-pound, six-footer with Buddy Holly horn-rimmed glasses. I put on my one suit and

> "When you have time, you can cover some games if you want to, and we'll get them in the paper if we have space."

arrived at his office at the appointed time. I was a kid and I was unprepared. I knew what I wanted to say, but I was not at all prepared for the consequences.

At some point in the brief conversation, I remember saying to him: "I've been working for you for a year, making $25 a week. I've got to have a raise, or else . . ."

I didn't know what "or else" was, but he did.

He rose from behind his huge desk and strode to the open door of an office adjoining his, and raising his voice just high enough for his accountant to hear, and said: "Make out Charlie's check. He's leaving us."

And thus ended my first newspaper job.

I learned the relative worth of sports and sportswriters in the course of one abortive sentence. It was a lesson I never forgot—and a story I got a lot of mileage from—as my career took me to newspapers in Taylor, Beaumont, Galveston, and San Antonio, Texas, then to Sandusky, Ohio, and finally to the *Detroit Free Press*.

Late in my career, I'd see young men and women come to work for one of the largest and best papers in the United States right out of college. I never envied them. I always figured they were missing part of their education by not working at the *Victoria Mirror,* or someplace like it.

... when you turn on that microphone, give it your best shot ...

My first play-by-play work was at WRAM in Monmouth, Illinois, from 1957 to 1960. The primary team was the football squad at Monmouth College, where I was a student.

To say the Fighting Scots were less than the best in those days would be very kind indeed.

Often while I was describing the woes on the gridiron, a young coach from Coe College would be in attendance scouting the Kohawks' next opponent. He would constantly kid me about making a 66-0 rout sound like a 6-6 tie.

That coach went his way and I went mine; occasionally we bumped into each other over the years when one of his basketball teams would play one of the teams I was covering.

By 1970, I decided sportscasting was not going to pay off for me, so I became station manager at a radio station in Terre Haute, Indiana. One day, I saw a small note in the local newspaper that the expansion Cleveland Cavaliers had named their first coach—Bill Fitch, the same coach I had known back in my Monmouth days.

I sent him a note of congratulations. Several days later, Coach Fitch called me with an invitation to come to Cleveland and audition for the Cavs' radio play-by-play job. With his blessings, I was given the job, and twenty-nine years later I'm still here.

Bottom line. No matter what point you are in your career, when you turn on that microphone, give it your best shot, because you never know who might be listening and remember.

Joe Tait has been the play-by-play voice for the Cleveland Cavaliers in the NBA for 29 years.

I wanted to ... become the nation's first Jewish spaceman.

Stu Bykofsky has been writing a four-times-weekly column in the *Philadelphia Daily News* since 1987.

The first thing I remember is the smell.

Not a delicate *odor*, but a *smell*, gorilla heavy and oddly sweet.

It was the smell of the syrup-like printer's ink slathered on the basement presses at the *World-Telegram & The Sun*, at 125 Barclay Street on New York's West Side, facing the Hudson River, which occasionally backed up, overflowed its banks, and poured into the basement, creating havoc for the newspaper.

At 8 A.M. on my first day of work, I passed the Greek-owned greasy spoon lurking at the front door (the restaurant had a few booths, but was mostly a Formica and fluorescent shoebox with stools covered in red vinyl and an overworked grill), pushed through the brass revolving door into the Telly, saw the oversized black bust of one of the founders (Scripps? Howard?, I forget) and smelled the ink coming from the pressroom, located behind the green door across from the elevator bank.

It was winter 1959 and I was starting my first journalism job as a copyboy at the now-defunct Telly.

It was the era of tan or black chinos (blue jeans were still for farmers) that had a buckle in the back, and sport shirts that could be madras or pink. It was an era when a copyboy (there were no copygirls yet) could work his way up to a reporter's job—even in New York. I was shown to a wooden bench where copyboys sat waiting for the first cry of "Copy!" that would send you racing to the reporter to grab his copy book (four sheets of cheap carbon paper interspersed among five sheets of low-grade copy paper). The bottom sheet stayed with the reporter; the others would be delivered to four editors. There were maybe eight kids ranging in age from seventeen—me—to twenty-eight, all white, who sat there.

We didn't mind the reporters yelling "Copy!" or "Copyboy!" but we hated the few who just yelled "Boy!" (That pretty much died a few years later when African Americans were hired and "boy" was viewed—wrongly in this case—as a racial stereotype. Sensitivity triumphed over tradition.)

I never set out to become a reporter. Entering high school in 1955, I wanted to be a nuclear physicist, go into the space program and become the nation's first Jewish spaceman. (I don't think the term "astronaut" had been coined yet.)

I took three years of physics in high school.

Unfortunately, it was a one-year course. I started to reconsider my career choice.

I always had a gift for writing, so I thought I'd join the high school newspaper. They told me my grades were too low, that I needed to concentrate more on my schooling. It was about this time the Russians launched Sputnik and America got serious about space, but I was just taking *up* space. No newspaper as an extracurricular activity? OK. I perfected my pool game.

I entered Brooklyn College night school not knowing a soul. I decided I should join some kind of club in order to meet people. When I say "people," what I mean, of course, is girls. I wasn't the type who'd join a fraternity. There were house plans (fraternities without the Greek letters and attitude), but they got to see girls only on Friday nights. Hmmm. What about the student newspaper? They got to see girls every night. And what did I know of reporters of that era? They smoked, they drank, they talked dirty.

I could handle that.

I joined the student newspaper. I had a gift. I excelled. The editor of the paper worked at the Telly. He got me a job there.

So there I am, walking in, and I remember the smell.

I remember some of the people, too.

There was the union rep named Robin Turkel, dark-haired, dark-skinned. He always wore blue Oxford button-down shirts and rep ties. He always had time to show a kid how to write or conjure up a lede.

There was Paul Meskill, a mole-like crackerjack crime reporter who wore a leather trenchcoat he had had made in Germany with a built-in shoulder holster. Great reporter. (But he yelled "Boy!") He went on to the *New York Daily News*.

There was Trudy Viner, a sleek brunette with great legs who was among the early female cityside reporters. I remember her flagging down a vegetable truck to give her a lift to a shooting when she couldn't find a

> "I decided I should join some kind of club in order to meet people. When I say 'people,' what I mean, of course, is girls."

cab. I guess I had a crush on her.

My favorite was news/feature writer Ed Wallace, a white-haired, Scottish imp who became my unofficial mentor. (In that era, no one would dare use a word like "mentor.")

He was a great wordsmith and a great idea man who taught me to think out an assignment before picking up a pencil. Wallace was given to wearing yellow-tinted shooting glasses in the newsroom. (He founded a club called "Friends of the Colt .45," a firearm he favored, and taught me to shoot, at the NYPD range.)

I remember the old teletype machines' bells ringing when an "urgent" came across. I remember large fans blowing copy paper everywhere (because there was no air-conditioning then). I remember the smoking, the hooch stored in reporters' lockers. I remember reporters sleeping on their desks when their wives threw them out. I remember the profanity. I remember nearly choking on the tickertape blizzard during a Wall Street parade for Richard Nixon. I remember hearing bullets whiz by during a riot I helped cover.

But mostly I remember the smell of the printer's ink.

I miss those days.

I miss that smell.

> "But mostly I remember the smell of the printer's ink."

I was going to do some hard-hitting journalism.

It was the Reagan years and Mr. Reagan had mentioned something about volunteerism, but that had nothing to do with why I took a job at $50 a week to report for KLWX, a public broadcasting station in Las Vegas.

Long before I got into sports reporting, I was going to do some hard-hitting journalism. To that end, I found myself on the Las Vegs strip, trying to pull off the definitive piece on prostitution. Trouble was, a lady of the night saw the wireless microphone I was wearing. Apparently, I didn't pose the same attack-dog scare that a *60 Minutes* crew would have. The woman went on the (verbal) attack against my cameramen and me. We were pretty certain her associates were on the way.

We abandoned our tripod and ran. After all, it was fifty bucks and no health insurance.

Kenny Mayne is a sportscaster for ESPN.

It was the excitement, the glamour I was in it for.

Doug Robarchek is a columnist for the *Charlotte (North Carolina) Observer.*

It was December 26, 1961, and Christmas had been an anticlimax. Today I was receiving a gift to last a lifetime: It was my first day on my first newspaper job at the *Grand Island (Nebraska) Daily Independent.*

The paper had hired me weeks before, but let me stay on my job at the Coast-to-Coast Drugstore and help them through the Christmas rush. I was eighteen and had been out of high school for seven months.

I was undereducated, undermotivated and almost perfectly innocent of any of the skills or knowledge required to be a good journalist (if "good journalist" isn't too jarring an oxymoron). In addition, I didn't type very well, I wasn't cursed with great ambition and my contact with reality was sometimes tenuous. I was born to be a columnist.

"Doug Robarchek," I kept thinking, "who, disguised as a mild-mannered reporter for a not-so-great, not-so-metropolitan newspaper, wages a never-ending battle for truth, justice and the American way." And sixty bucks a week. Think of it as a get-rich-quick scheme.

Naw, who needed money? Grand Island was home. I could live at my parents' house. It was the excitement, the glamour I was in it for. There's that reality problem again.

I made up my mind I would save the first thing I ever wrote that was published in the paper. I would frame it, and years later, when I was a famous newspaperman, it would hang on the wall of my office amid the honorary degrees and the Pulitzers.

It would be cool if it was something exciting. A really good story. A murder was probably too much to hope for (especially since Grand Island probably didn't average a murder a decade), but I wasn't greedy. I'd settle for a good armed robbery, preferably with a hail of bullets. I had never seen an actual hail of bullets. Or even a drizzle of bullets, for that matter.

The city editor, a gruff, crew-cut ex-Marine named Ernie Hines, put me right to work. He had me phone the hospitals for the lists of admissions and dismissals. In a town like Grand Island, which of your friends and neighbors were going into and coming out of the hospital was news.

And that was my first story in the newspaper: "Admitted Tuesday at St.

Francis Hospital: John Doe, Jane Smith, etc."

I decided not to save it and frame it. That was my first lesson that newspapering might not be all glory.

But, hey, I was in the door, at the tail end of a time when reporting was still a trade and you could break into it like a steamfitter or a carpenter, without going to college.

Newspapers were hot type and manual typewriters and paste pots and middle-aged white men. And a wonderful revolution was coming like a fresh wind off the sea to change all that forever, and I had hitched on for the ride.

But even with all their faults, I loved the old newsrooms of little afternoon papers, where the day started at 5:30 A.M. and you hit the ground running, sometimes without having been to bed the night before, and you worked on massive doses of coffee and cigarettes.

It was a time when the newsroom was almost as sacrosanct a male preserve as the pool hall, and there was a fire in the wastebasket at least once a week from somebody emptying an ashtray that still had live coals in it, and old news hounds really did get drunk on the job. (Larry S. used to get drunker and drunker as the afternoon wore on, and we couldn't figure out where he was getting it. Finally, somebody followed him when he went for coffee, and found he had a bottle in the toilet tank in the composing room john.)

I couldn't know it that first day, but over the years ahead, newspapers all over the country would show me things horrible and wonderful, introduce me to most of my best friends in life, and provide a pretty fair free education to a small-town kid who was too aimless to go to college.

"In a town like Grand Island, which of your friends and neighbors were going into and coming out of the hospital was news."

... he snarled, ... "You're fired, kid. Get outta here."

George Vecsey is a sports columnist on The New York Times *and the author of several books.*

Some days it was liverwurst. Some days it was ham. Some days it was bologna.

As far as I could see, the deli run was the most important thing I did at my first job at a newspaper. I certainly never learned one thing remotely connected to "reporting" or "editing" or whatever it was men did in the sports department in the *New York Daily News* in the summers of 1956 and 1957.

In those pre-computer days, I was a copyboy. My boss was a pasty, bleak tyrant named Charlie Hoerter. He was a bit inscrutable. He would creep up silently behind me to the wire machines and glance down at the paper copy humming out of their innards, and he would say something like, "He's a great player."

"Who, Charlie?"

"That Gordie Howe."

There was absolutely no hockey on the wires in midsummer, but whatever.

Our most personal contact came around 6 P.M., when he would send me out to the delicatessen on Second Avenue for some kind of cold cut sandwich and a container of beer. It had to be a cardboard container, so it would look as if Charlie was sipping iced tea, not that anybody was fooled.

Charlie was harmless enough until the first edition was wrapped up, and then he would wander out into the evening. If you were lucky, he would not come back. Occasionally, he would materialize around 9 P.M. looking like a very perturbed Ahab in search of some hapless white whale.

One night he fixed those terrible red eyes on me and snarled, "You're fired, kid. Get outta here." Then he lurched on down the hallway to who knows where.

Having no personal belongings to gather up, I said a hasty good-bye to a few solicitous souls and prepared to leave forever.

"Where are you going?" asked Ed Hurley.

"Just stay out of sight if he comes back," said Hughie Barber.

"He won't remember a thing tomorrow," said Wes Gaffer.

"Besides which, the heck with him," said Red Foley.

It was absolutely true. The next day Charlie muttered, "Hey, kid," and life went on.

There were glimmers of awe about working at the *Daily News*. In the looming lobby, there was a giant globe, reminding us of human activity outside the doors. It was midsummer, people were at the beach, going on picnics, taking the night air in parks. The globe shimmered. Up in the sports department, men hunched over pieces of paper and made paragraph marks.

The *Daily News* sold billions of papers every day, wherever the trucks and trains could carry them. By sheer circulation alone, the newspaper was a force. Its general tone was, essentially, "Hang 'em High"—Commies, Pinkos, Lefties, rascals, troublemakers, anybody suspicious. I always felt the editorial tone permeated the ozone of the tall building on 42nd Street.

From my menial corner of the sports department, I never heard "journalism" discussed, or tangibly practiced, but that was fine, because both my parents were journalists and we talked about things at home. My father, George Vecsey, had once been the sports editor of a Newhouse paper, the *Long Island Press*, until he took a union stand, and his assistant got his job. Now he worked for The Associated Press full-time, but filled in two nights a week on the *Daily News* copy desk, and had gotten me this job paying $1.20 an hour.

The other men in the department treated my father with great respect. They knew he knew things. If I did something goofy, they would sigh and say, "Your father is such a great guy."

Those summers, I did learn a few things that would help me in life.

I learned agility. I would be dispatched to the composing room, where great metal pages were being assembled. While I waited for an editor to hand me the proofs, I would hear the words, "Look out, college boy," and I would spot a born assassin pushing a lethal steel cart at breakneck speed down the narrow aisle. If I did not react immediately, he would kill me.

I learned hope. If I prayed hard enough, the *Daily News*'s star woman reporter, Kitty Hanson, would sashay down the corridor toward the city room. I remember her as mature, with reddish hair, summery dresses, wide-brimmed hats—or maybe I have confused her with Brenda Starr—and a trace of a smile that said a) she had a

> "I learned hope. If I prayed hard enough, the *Daily News*'s star woman reporter, Kitty Hanson, would sashay down the corridor toward the city room."

good story to write and b) she knew that lost boys like me were gaping at her from our dismal cubbyholes. They didn't have women like that in my neighborhood in Queens.

I learned reality. Our copyeditors would come back from a late liquid dinner and tell about the latest brawl involving well-known players from the Milwaukee Braves and other visiting baseball teams.

I also learned to dream. The star of the *Daily News* sports department was Dick Young, who covered the Brooklyn Dodgers and made games come alive, and peppered his copy with pungent tabloid nicknames ("Skoonj" for Carl Furillo, who allegedly moved as slowly as a scungilli) and great baseball slang ("ribbies," for runs batted in) and had been one of the first baseball writers to ask provocative questions of players and managers in their fetid clubhouses.

Young had the charisma and the stubbornness of Frank Sinatra, whom he would imitate in the annual baseball writers' talent show. He dressed in snappy sports jackets and was always well-groomed. When he breezed into the office once a week or so, he would bring with him the tumult of the stands at Ebbets Field, the clatter of the railroad trains, the solid crack of a line drive, the rattle of a portable typewriter.

He also talked. He chatted with Carrie, the kind lady who ran the office. He chatted with my father, respectfully. He chatted with me. A lot of the top writers would collect their mail without taking time to acknowledge the hired hands who were just dying for a whiff of the outside world. Dick Young, on the other hand, knew my name, and had time for questions.

"How's Robinson's knee?" I would ask.

"He'll be out another week or two," he would say.

That would satisfy me. Dick Young instinctively created a link between the sunlit world where he excelled and the cave where we plodded.

After that second summer, I was lucky to find part-time work at *Newsday*, the great emerging paper on Long Island. Within two years, when I was twenty, I was covering the odd Yankee game. Young's Dodgers having deserted him for Los Angeles, he would spot me at Yankee Stadium and

> "A lot of the top writers would collect their mail without taking time to acknowledge the hired hands who were just dying for a whiff of the outside world."

introduce me to other reporters and ballplayers and managers. "Hey, Birdie, here's a new kid from *Newsday*. He's OK."

In his later years, when we were both columnists, Dick Young would take positions and behave in ways that I could not admire, but we were always cordial to each other. I remembered the man who had time for the copyboys.

They don't have copyboys any more, or even copygirls or copypersons. They're called "clerks" and they are not supposed to go out on food runs for editors. Democracy has come to journalism. The clerks at *The New York Times,* where I now work, hear zealous journalism being practiced all around them—meetings, conferences, ad hoc discussions, phone calls, urgent shouts across desktops, dozens of professionals working at their craft, consciously and collectively making the section better, punctuation mark by punctuation mark.

Believe me, it is no effort to talk with our clerks, because they are good people with a lot to offer. But when I visit our office, I always remember the lost and inarticulate evenings of those ancient summers, and the writer who made me want to try this business.

Sensing that this would be a mismatch, I argued against the game.

Gordon Forbes is professional football editor for *USA Today*. He has covered the NFL for thirty-three years and was selected to the Pro Football Hall of Fame in 1986.

A young man watches Gordon Forbes at work.

I covered high school sports for the *Florida Times-Union* in Jacksonville in the early 1960s. A new school, Terry Parker High, went unbeaten in its first season and challenged one of the city's powers, Jackson High, to a post-season game. Sensing that this would be a mismatch, given Jackson's superior size and experience and Terry Parker's youth and light weight, I argued against the game.

The day my column appeared, I was strung up in effigy on the Parker campus. Fortunately, the Parker kids didn't realize that I lived a short quarter-mile away in the Arlington section with a much closer tree.

When he waved the towel once, I started the interview.

In 1962, I was a member of the Milwaukee Braves broadcast team. One of my first post-game interviews was at the Polo Grounds in New York after a game with the Mets. That was before you had any communication between the announcer on the field and the associate producer in the broadcast booth. It was a pretty good distance, too, so here's how we worked it out: I stood with my guest around the home-plate area looking toward the booth. The associate producer had a towel in his hand. When he waved the towel once, I started the interview. After a couple of minutes, I had to keep glancing out of the corner of my eye at the booth, because two waves of the towel was my cue to go to commercial.

They've come a long way in terms of producing post-game shows.

Ernie Johnson pitched for the Boston Braves, the Milwaukee Braves and the Baltimore Orioles. He has broadcast Braves' games for thirty-five years on TV and radio.

Other than that, my first coverage assignment was uneventful.

Hal McCoy is a baseball writer on the *Dayton Daily News*. A former national president of the Baseball Writers Association of America, he has covered one team (the Cincinnati Reds) continuously longer than anybody else in the country.

I have asked, conservatively, twenty thousand questions in my job. But the first question I ever asked as a baseball writer still burns my ears and makes me shudder.

I was fired up and ready to cover my first game, but I wasn't yet the main beat writer. I was the regular guy's backup and was on my first assignment in 1967. After the game, a 2-1 Cincinnati victory over the Dodgers, I went to manager Dave Bristol's office.

At the time, pitcher Gary Nolan was battling arm problems and was supposed to throw on the side during the game. Regular beat writer Jim Ferguson instructed me, "Be sure to check on Nolan."

So, as all the writers filed into Bristol's office, I popped my first big-league question: "How did Nolan throw?"

Bristol, a tough and intimidating guy, arose from behind his desk, walked close to my face, stuck a finger in it and said, "We just won a great bleeping ball game against a great bleeping team and the first question you ask is about a hurt bleeping pitcher. That's a horse-bleep question. Next question."

Needless to say, "next question" was not from me, nor did I ask any others. It took several days to build up courage enough to ask another, and I made certain it was something like, "What day is it?" Something easy.

Years later, when Bristol returned as a coach with the Reds and I recounted how he had frightened the daylights out of a raw rookie reporter, he laughed and said, "I loved to intimidate young guys like you. I'd never do that to a veteran, even if he asked me the same question."

Thanks, Dave.

My first assignment of any kind for the old *Dayton Journal Herald,* fresh out of Kent State University J-school in 1962, was to cover a high school football game in Troy, Ohio.

After the game, I did my interviews and strolled back to the press box. I took my time, trying to make my first game-coverage story good. Just as I finished on my old Olivetti portable, all the lights went out in the press box, and everybody but me was gone. I couldn't see a thing. I stretched a telephone cord as far as it would go and went outside the press box on a landing and under a streetlight, where I dictated my story.

Then I packed up to leave and discovered that I was locked in the stadium, forcing me to climb a fifteen-foot gate with barbed wire on top. Yes, I ripped my brand new pants purchased that day for my assignment and sprained my left ankle jumping off the top of the gate.

Other than that, my first coverage assignment was uneventful.

> "I stretched a telephone cord as far as it would go and went outside the press box on a landing and under a streetlight, where I dictated my story."

I've never before or since been as petrified as I was that Sunday.

B. Peter Carry is executive editor of *Sports Illustrated*.

Nowadays, it would be called an internship, but back in 1961 it was just a summer job. I'd get $40 bucks a week ($14 of which went for a room at the Y) to fill in for vacationing reporters at the *Sun-Bulletin,* the morning paper in the upstate New York city of Binghamton. Since grammar school, I'd worked for every amateur publication that would have me, but this hot Sunday in early June of the summer between my freshman and sophomore years in college would be my first day as a pro. I arrived in the city room at 2 P.M., received a limp greeting from the executive editor who had hired me sight unseen and the city editor who would be my boss, and immediately was handed a slip of paper with a female's name and phone number on it.

She was the high school valedictorian, and her parents had given her one of those little British roadsters for graduation, I was told by way of explanation of the name and number. The previous night was the prom, and in the wee hours the little sports car had been driven under the trailer of a semi. The girl and her date had been decapitated. The paper had pictures of the crash scene but needed a portrait of the girl. Call the number and ask her parents for a photo.

A few months later, I would be scared to death when JFK announced the blockade of Cuba, and in a few years I'd be plenty fearful when the North Vietnamese started shooting at me and my shipmates, but I've never before or since been as petrified as I was that Sunday. As I searched through my desk as slowly as possible for paper and pencil, as I ambled off to the men's room to pretend to take a pee, as I looked out the window with hopes of seeing the tornado that would level the newspaper's building and lift this burden from me, I kept saying to myself, *What the hell are you going to do when this girl's father cusses you out for shamelessly intruding on the family's mourning, when her mother excoriates you for being an insensitive bastard?*

I happened to glance toward the front of the room and saw—or, at least, I thought I saw—the city editor looking grimly at me. With all deliberateness, I picked up the phone and dialed. Please be busy. It rang. Please, let there be no one at home. A somber man's voice answered. It was the girl's father. I apologized for calling and stammered out a request for a picture. I would come pick it up. He said there would be no need, that he would bring the picture in. Fifteen minutes later, the father showed up at my desk, introduced himself and handed me a portrait of his daughter in her cap and gown, which he had torn from her yearbook. Then he said, "Thank you," and walked away.

> "The previous night was the prom, and in the wee hours the little sports car had been driven under the trailer of a semi."

... a major mob figure had been shot dead while in a barber chair.

Bruce Morton is a news reporter for CNN. He formerly worked for ABC News in London and CBS News in Washington, D.C.

I wrote newscasts for a local radio station in college, but my first real news job was as a flunky for a New York TV station. The big story one day was that a major mob figure had been shot dead while in a barber chair at a downtown hotel. I was sent to the Manhattan West police station where I watched throngs of plainclothes detectives, suspects, etc., file in and out. All were new faces to me. I finally asked a print veteran how you could tell the crooks from the cops.

He answered kindly, "The cops are the ones who need haircuts."

Live and learn.

... he told me I was violating Guild rules ...

The *Huntington Park (California) Daily Signal* was a small, suburban daily when I was hired as a vacation relief reporter in the summer of 1963. At summer's end, the editor asked me to stay on full-time and agreed to arrange a work schedule around my school schedule. To make things a little easier, he gave me Fridays off in exchange for working a half day on Saturday.

Two months later—on Friday, November 22, 1963—I walked into my Shakespeare class at UCLA and heard the first report that President Kennedy had been shot. Day off or not, I raced from the classroom, jumped into my car and drove at breakneck speed to the *Signal* office.

The paper only had three editors and four reporters, so the editors were glad to see me, even as green as I was, and they immediately put me to work getting local reaction over the phone. But the *Signal* belonged to the American Newspaper Guild, and ten minutes later, the union shop steward asked me to accompany him to the men's room, where—standing in front of the urinal next to me—he told me I was violating Guild rules by coming to work on my day off.

"Go home," he said.

Summoning all the restraint in my twenty-year-old body, I zipped up before turning to face him. I looked at him and said, "Let me get this straight. I'm a brand-new reporter, the president of the United States has just been assassinated, we're shorthanded and you're telling me to go home."

He nodded vigorously.

I shook my head even more vigorously. "You must be fucking nuts," I said. Then I marched back out to the newsroom and resumed my work.

David Shaw is a Pulitzer Prize-winning media critic for the *Los Angeles Times*.

"... type it right the first time, or don't bother finishing your shift."

Art Thiel is sports columnist on the *Seattle Post-Intelligencer*. He has been voted Washington's Sportswriter of the Year five times.

The idea of working for the *Tacoma (Washington) News Tribune* seemed bigtime, because I had grown up reading the newspaper, knew all the bylines, and figured, hey, I can do this sportswriting job.

During my freshman year, the newspaper called the college paper needing part-time help to take the Friday night prep scores. I figured this was my chance.

The building was a classic *Front Page* shambles, full of pitted wood floors, creaky walks that rattled with the press run, and the smell of ink, cigarettes and sweat (no air conditioning). The writer in charge of training the prep dweebs put me down in front of an old Underwood upright and told me to answer the phone and type in whatever I was told onto tri-carbon paper.

Nervous, I took the first call from a football coach who was savvy enough to dictate the linescore and scoring summary exactly as the form required. I wasn't good enough to type it that way. By the time he gave me notes for a story, I had a mess and was behind what seemed like years. As soon as I hung up, an editor snatched the paper from my typewriter.

"This is it?" he growled. Well, no, I replied. I would have to type up a fresh summary because I, uh, didn't get a few things.

"I guess you don't get it, kid," he said. "This is a daily newspaper, not some term paper. You've got to type it right the first time, or don't bother finishing your shift."

My dead panic was interrupted by another prep call. This time it was the scorekeeper's daughter phoning a result. It was her first time, too, and she was more scared than I was. I had to talk her through the form so slowly that I could type along. As soon as the labored conversation ended, the editor again ripped my copy from the typewriter. It was clean.

"Better," he mumbled, walking away. "Quit spending so much time on the phone with these people."

"OK," I said, voice cracking. It was years before I realized I owed my entire newspaper career to some anonymous fourteen-year-old who was so scared she kept me from running out of the building and into bartending.

Tom Harmon was leaving Channel 2 and recommended me ...

My start was easy. I realized that a big sports name would open doors for a fledgling sportscaster, and the route I pursued was as a baseball umpire. After five years in Class C leagues, I finally graduated to the Pacific Coast League in 1952. The late Tom Harmon was leaving his nightly spot on Channel 2 and recommended me to replace him. He explained to the program director that I had been an actor in movies and TV (*Stalag 17*, *The Wild One* and *That's My Boy*), so I knew the camera and mikes, plus as a PCL ump I had the sports background.

And I've broadcasted ever since, graduating to assignments at the Rome Olympics, doing play-by-play for the Los Angeles Rams and feature races at Santa Anita and Hollywood Park.

Gil Stratton retired from CBS Sports after forty-three years.

... was whether the dead person was worth a whole obituary ...

Roger Simon writes about politics for *U.S. News & World Report.*

It was 1970, I was just out of college, and I had just started work at the City News Bureau of Chicago. It was a place with a lot of famous alumni such as Kurt Vonnegut and Mike Royko and Seymour Hersh. It also was a place that specialized in tragedy.

Every day I would go to a different police station and do stories on murders, rapes and armed robberies. I would report on human misery. In other words, the kind of thing that fills newspapers.

One of my jobs at City News was to check out coroners' cases. Anybody who was not in a doctor's care when he died was such a case. The desk at City News would get a report from the coroner, it would be passed along to me, and I would call the survivors to find out about the dead person.

But what I was really trying to find out was whether the dead person was worth a whole obituary or not. Whether he was a somebody or a nobody. If he was a nobody, I would, in a journalistic term I have never forgotten, "cheap him out," and no story would be done. You could not waste a lot of time on a nobody. You had a lot of coroners' cases to get through each day.

"Mr. Smith was a bricklayer?" you would ask the widow. "A very good bricklayer. Yes, how nice. And you? A housewife? Yes, how nice."

And you'd call back to the desk and tell them that they would not have to worry about Arthur Smith, beloved husband of Irma, devoted father of John, Paulette, and Arthur Jr. He was just another of God's creatures. And his passing was nothing we had to worry about. Or even take notice of.

There was a whole list of facts to check first, of course. Not just the deceased's job, but whether he was a member of any civic organizations or fraternal lodges. And—my personal favorite—whether he had been awarded any significant military decorations. For if he had been fortunate enough to have killed the requisite number of human beings in some past conflict, he might be elevated in death from obscurity to ten lines of type in a newspaper.

Every day I would call the grief-stricken. The shattered widows. Sobbing widowers. Stunned children. Speechless parents. I had my spiel down. I knew which words to emphasize and which words to hurry over to give the impression that I was on official business.

"City News Bureau calling. The Cook County Coroner's Office has made a report and we need to check some facts."

I was always amazed that it worked. That the grieving would tell me whatever I asked, that they would rummage through the dusty drawers of their lives for a stranger on the telephone.

"A veteran, was he? Ever awarded the Medal of Honor? Distingushed Service Cross? Silver Star? Are you sure? Could you check?"

And then one day a woman laughed. This was a first. I had heard choked sobs. Angry silences. And, once, a scream. But never a laugh.

"That's my husband's name, all right," she said. "But he isn't dead. He went out for a paper. He's fine. At least last I looked." And she laughed again.

I laughed with her. And apologized. And called back to the desk to report that an error had been made.

"No, wait, can't be," the desk said. A riffle of papers. "Must be a fresh one. This guy was run over on, lemme see, South Jeffrey Avenue. She must not know yet."

And so I knew what she did not. That her husband was not coming back with that paper. That he was in a sliding drawer at the Cook County Morgue with a tag on his toe.

So what am I supposed to do now? I asked.

"What do you mean, what do you do now?" said the desk. "You call her back and tell her that her husband is dead and you have some questions. What—I got to explain everything?"

When I tell this story among friends, I usually pause. And wait. And if the people around me aren't newspaper people, they always ask the same thing.

"So what did you do?"

"You didn't really call her back, did you? I mean, not really."

"You didn't, did you?"

If they are newspaper people, however, they never ask. They know I called her back. And told her it was me again from City News, and I hated to be the one to break the news, but the Cook County Coroner's Office had made this report, and, well, I needed to check some facts. Such as the deceased's profession. Civic organizations. Fraternal lodges. And, by the way, had he ever been given any significant military decorations?

He hadn't, by the way.

I cheaped him out.

> "If he was a nobody, I would, in a journalistic term I have never forgotten, 'cheap him out,' and no story would be done."

Student after student tried out, each getting five to ten minutes ...

Kevin Harlan is a sportscaster for CBS Sports and Turner Sports.

During my sophomore year at Premontre High School in Green Bay, Wisconsin, they were holding try-outs for the play-by-play job at our student-run, ten-watt FM radio station. Football season was just two weeks away. It was an all-boys Catholic school, so nuns and priests taught classes. And nuns and priests would select the announce team.

Tryouts were held in a classroom, a film from a previous game was shown on the chalkboard, and we were to talk into a tape recorder. Student after student tried out, each getting five to ten minutes. At fourteen, I was the youngest applicant.

I began to watch the film and felt comfortable. During the game, there was a fumble and a big pile on top of the loose ball. As the officials were clearing players, one of our players began jumping up and down indicating that perhaps our team had recovered the ball. My call went something like this . . . "The players are getting off the pile, no indication as to who has recovered the fumble . . . wait a minute, the Cadets appear to have it. Joe Ehlinger is jumping up and down for ovulation . . ."

Now either history was being made, or I was in for a short broadcasting career. There was silence in the room. I really hadn't realized what I had said. Then one by one each priest and nun began laughing. Finally, it dawned on me. Not ovulation, you idiot, but jubilation. He was jumping up and down for jubilation.

I guess they thought anything that unpredictable would be worth listening to, and I got the job. And from that moment on, I knew that play-by-play was for me.

My first newspaper job started with an act of omission or a lie ...

My first newspaper job started with an act of omission or a lie, depending on your viewpoint. I filled out an internship application for the *Philadelphia Bulletin,* the city's large afternoon daily. As the electronic banner on the outside of the building announced to the world, "Nearly Everybody Reads the *Bulletin.*" Based on clippings from my high school paper and stringer work I'd done for a paper in upstate New York, my application was accepted.

But I had intentionally not included my age or a picture of my eighteen-year-old face, because the internship was limited to college seniors and graduate students. When I showed up on the first day of work, the editors looked at me and said: You are not a senior or grad student.

After informing me that they were not a baby-sitting service and making noises about me being tricky and slick by not entering my age, they asked me to leave. Luckily for me, one of my professors at Haverford College called the editors and argued that the writing samples were mine and they should give me a two-week tryout. I was back at work the next day. Two weeks passed, three weeks passed and no one ever mentioned the problem again. In fact, they invited me to work there during the school year.

Juan Williams is an award-winning columnist on the *Washington Post.*

The victim's husband was the prime suspect. A doctor of some sort.

Jack Perkins, a former TV newsman, makes frequent appearances on the Arts & Entertainment Network.

I had gotten the job as a fluke. For eight years, radio station WGAR in Cleveland had been co-sponsoring with Western Reserve University a speech contest for high school seniors. First prize was a full four-year scholarship to Reserve and a job at the station. Eight years they'd been doing this, but each year the winner, bound for some other school in some other town, declined the prizes.

Well, when my turn came, I accepted. Which presented WGAR a dilemma: What to do with this kid from Wooster, Ohio, with no particular training or background.

"I could always use somebody to change paper in the wire machines," piped Charlie Day, station news director. Thus was a career determined, a journalist born.

It was three years later, while doing the Sunday morning newscasts, that I got a tip from a police friend. A murder had been discovered out in suburban Bay Village. The victim's husband was the prime suspect. A doctor of some sort. Dr. Sam Sheppard.

His case and the raucous trial it spawned became the judicial sensation (if not scandal) of the era, complete with the suspect-harboring family, the unknown bushy-haired intruder (later, in TV's ripoff, to become the "one-armed man," furtively pursued by "The Fugitive").

For two years, that case dominated news in this nation, and a certain college student was too busy with his job to be taking care of business on campus.

Oh, it worked out fine. When the trial finally wrapped and I bolted from the courtroom to dash to the live microphone we had secreted in a courtroom closet down the hall, I was the first on the air with the verdict—scooping the competition, which included one of my own professors who did news on a local TV channel.

That didn't bode well for my immediate college career. In fact, that semester, at the height of my preoccupation with the Sheppard case, I found myself on campus being elected student council president and then six weeks later being removed from office for never attending a single student council meeting. That semester, while being inducted into Omicron Delta Kappa, the honorary society for outstanding scholars, my grades were three F's, a D, and a W (for withdrawn). It took five and a half years to get through four years of college, but who cared. Sometimes the best education doesn't come from education.

> "For two years, that case dominated news in this nation, and a certain college student was too busy with his job to be taking care of business on campus."

... the station was behind in paying me. Six weeks to be exact.

Marc Zumoff is the television voice of the Philadelphia '76ers in the National Basketball Association.

The all-news station in Trenton, New Jersey, was in trouble. WBUD-AM had lost its primary feeder service, NIS. This service supplied most of the station's programming by sending news and information to WBUD and a host of affiliates, making up the bulk of their on-air product. After NIS failed, WBUD tried to maintain the all-news format utilizing a miniscule staff. My first job came courtesy of WBUD in July of 1977, ripping and reading wire copy and bringing in NBC network feeds to round out the presentation.

At $110 a week, I worked from 6 A.M. to 9 A.M., took a three-hour break, and then came back and worked noon to 3 P.M. While I was thrilled at the prospect of getting paid to do something I loved, the station was behind in paying me. Six weeks to be exact. In addition, it was operating on antique equipment that was constantly in disrepair. Frequently I'd be reading the news only to discover I'd been off the air for the last ten or fifteen minutes.

Since this was my first job, I dealt with the adverse conditions. Finally, though, my patience was tested to the limit. I decided that the six-week lag in pay and frequent off-the-air episodes were enough. So I summoned the courage to tell the station owner, an overweight, crusty old man who employed only one management person, his lady program director.

One day I marched to his office, emboldened by the fact that the station was off the air; I figured he'd want to know. I knocked on his door several times, but there was no answer, even though I knew he was in his office. In fact, when I cupped my ear to the door, I heard people inside. Finally, I knocked a third time and heard him yell, "What is it?"

I told him the station was off the air. I listened but heard nothing. So I knocked and repeated the news.

Still nothing. I then leaned against the unlatched door and it slowly opened. Wide-eyed, I watched in wonder as the station owner and his lady program director wrestled passionately, partially clothed and fully involved, on the top of his desk. I quickly closed the door, but before I could turn away, the lady program director yelled, "What the hell do you want?"

I sheepishly responded.

"Well, Marc," the woman said, "maybe he wants it that way."

At least I didn't have to move back into the housing projects ...

I will always remember my first editor, Nancy Q. Keefe.

First of all, she hired me. This was in the fall of 1980 when I was feeling pretty dejected. And who wouldn't? There I was, a native New Yorker, a homegirl, who couldn't get hired by the *New York Daily News, The New York Times* or the *Staten Island Advance.*

"Not seasoned enough," a crusty *Times* editor said.

The one reporting job I was offered in Jersey City was tempting, but it paid less than $200 a week. I wasn't feeling arrogant when I turned the job down, I was being practical. You see, on that funny money I wouldn't have been able to pay my rent, my car note, George Washington Bridge tolls and still have a few bucks left over to eat.

Were I a kid living at home, maybe.

But I was thirty-four years old. How was I supposed to get my parents to understand that after eight years of attending college, mostly at night, and earning two degrees, including a master's from Columbia University's Graduate School of Journalism, no respectable hometown paper would hire me, while another across the river couldn't even afford to match the salaries I had earned for years as a secretary with just a high school diploma?

So, to me, Nancy Keefe, now retired, but at the time editor of Gannett's now-defunct *Daily Argus* in Mount Vernon, New York, was a goddess. The $250 a week she offered wasn't great, but it was doable. At least I didn't have to move back into the housing projects where I lived as a girl.

Nancy was a tough and caring editor, just the sort a beginning reporter needs. I'll always remember the day she jumped up from editing one of my stories, crossed our little newsroom in what seemed a single bound, planted herself directly in my face and bellowed, "There's no such word as 'irregardless'!"

Betty Winston Bayé is an editorial writer/columnist for the *Louisville Courier-Journal.* Her columns are syndicated by the Gannett News Service.

We even had an editor whose title was "assistant nipple chipper."

Elaine Viets is a nationally syndicated columnist and the author of *The Pink Flamingo Murders*.

When I graduated from college, I offered the *St. Louis Post-Dispatch* a real bargain: Woodward and Bernstein, rolled into one.

The *Post* hired me, all right. As a fashion writer.

I had two qualifications: I was a woman and I wore clothes.

The first one almost undid me. During my interview, the editor asked a question that is now illegal. He said: "Are you planning to have children?"

I fixed him a sorrowful look and said: "Oh, sir, I'm sterile."

He blushed to his hair roots. And since he was going bald, they went pretty far back. Then he patted me on the hand. "There, there, dear," he said. "Medical science has made many advances."

And so my fashion career started, based on the first of many misunderstandings.

I was writing fashion in the dreaded jersey era. This was in the early 1970s, when dresses, especially evening dresses, were made of clinging jersey. Jersey shows every mole, bump and nipple. Especially nipple. If a nipple got into the newspaper, strong male editors would scream and faint.

We even had an editor whose title was "assistant nipple chipper." Not officially, of course. He worked in the society section. But if one of the high editors thought he saw a nipple, and it was too late to remake the picure, the nipple chipper had to run down to the composing room and literally chisel the offending nipple off the metal. That way, the public didn't see a nipple in the newspaper. They saw a gray blob that looked like someone had gorped on the woman's dress.

It wasn't easy being a fashion writer in the jersey era. My stories had to show the fashionable new dresses. Most were cut so the model couldn't wear a bra. She also couldn't show a nipple. The solution was to have the models wear Band-Aids. That just about covered the subject for most models anyway. But I admired those women. Ripping off that Band-Aid was incredibly painful. Still, I didn't offer to kiss it and make it better.

When the models were made up for fashion shoots, they looked beautiful. They were also beautiful in real life. The only comfort I had was that they were miserable while they worked. Not only did they have Band-Aids on their breasts, their sleeves were stuffed with scratchy tags, their shoe soles were protected with slippery masking tape—and for instant tailoring, their outfits were pulled back with wooden clothespins.

From behind, the clothespins traveled up their spines like wooden vertebrae. In the oven-hot St. Louis summers, they had to wear heavy wool and fur fall fashions. In the bitter cold, they had to be photographed in thin summer clothes.

And not shiver, sweat or look unhappy.

I never envied them.

They never envied me either.

There were other traps awaiting me. The newspaper changed fashion writers back then the way you change socks. Some of these young women were free spirits, indeed. After I was hired, I showed up at a snooty store and introduced myself to the fashion coordinator as the new fashion writer.

She looked me up and down and said, "Well, at least you wear shoes."

I couldn't figure out what the old bat meant. Later I discovered one fashion writer wore the latest "gypsy" style from New York—and showed up for an interview at the store barefoot.

Some of my troubles I made for myself. Like the time I ran off to cover the Jean Patou trunk show without checking the files for background on the designer.

"And how is Mr. Patou?" I asked the company representative, chummily.

"Dead. For thirty years," she said, at her iciest. She was almost as cold as Mr. Patou.

At least I picked up the fashion lingo quickly.

When it was a dull season, I wrote

> "'And how is Mr. Patou?' I asked the company representative, chummily. 'Dead. For thirty years,' she said …"

stories about "the return of the classics."

When it was an incredibly dull season, I wrote: "Thank goodness designers are making real clothes for real women."

What were those other clothes for? Unreal women?

Actually, yes. Models in the early 1970s were emaciated. Human coat hangers. If they had generous figures, they would detract from the clothes. One of the strangest sights was backstage at a New York showing. The models were rushing around changing, when a TV crew came through. Here was a roomful of young women with gorgeous, bony faces, wearing only sheer-to-the-waist panty hose. The all-male camera crew didn't even give them a second look. They treated them like the coat hangers they were.

It was a New York show that ended my fashion career. I went to New York for the spring and fall shows. Each season had its own color. That fall, I saw three thousand plum dresses. Next spring, it was three thousand navy dresses.

And the next fall, another three thousand dresses. The announcer came up to the podium and said dramatically, "This year, Oscar de la Renta believes in gray."

I was the only one in the room who laughed. I knew it was time for a change.

> "The all-male camera crew didn't even give them a second look. They treated them like the coat hangers they were."

... he said only, "We have copy aides here in their mid-thirties."

I was fresh out of graduate school and just married when I realized it was time to get a job, sooner rather than later. I'd been a teenage copyreader at the Bell Syndicate in New York, and a copyboy (they still called us that in the '50s) at the *Milwaukee Sentinel,* but now I wanted to be a reporter, in New York City where I grew up.

My first interview was at the AP, where the kindly bureau chief liked me well enough to suggest he might recommend me for an outlying bureau, but said there were, alas, no openings for beginners in the Big Apple. Next stop was *The New York Times,* where the city editor, Arthur Gelb, told me he might find me a spot as a copy aide (*The Times* had started using that description, as I recall it). When I asked how long it would take before I could try out as a reporter, he said only, "We have copy aides here in their mid-thirties." So I said, thanks, but I'll keep looking.

I was getting a bit discouraged by now, but hope revived when a letter to *Time* magazine produced an invitation to come in for an interview. I arrived eagerly, only to be sent to the personnel department. Some rather stuffed-shirt greeted me, inspected my credentials and tsk-tsked the paucity of my reporting experience.

At *Time,* he informed me, "we want people who have a nose for news." I couldn't resist. "At *Time,*" I replied, "I would think that's the last thing you'd need. All you do is copy the front page of *The New York Times* every week and add a few details."

Needless to say, I didn't get any kind of offer from *Time.* With my bride growing more impatient by the day, I decided to say good-bye to my home town and plunged into the *Editor & Publisher Yearbook* for places to try. A few weeks later, I was hired at the Worcester, Massachusetts, *Telegram,* doing night rewrite on the 5 P.M. to 2 A.M. shift for $75 a week. It was a great place to begin, especially since it gave me time to learn how to type without hunting and pecking. They didn't seem to mind at all when I brought my typing manual to work, but before long, they put me on the night city desk where I didn't have to do much typing at all.

George Lardner of the *Washington Post* won the 1993 Pulitzer Prize for feature-writing.

Yes, you already caught that, I was on the society desk.

Georgie Anne Geyer is a nationally syndicated columnist.

It was January of 1959 when I faced my first day of work at the old *Chicago Daily News,* and I was filled with anticipation. The *Daily News* was one of our greatest of papers in those days, the paper of Carl Sandburg, Ben Hecht and Ernest Hemingway. It had always been a citadel of great writing, of soaring talents and of a very special kind of colleagueship. I was just out of Northwestern University, and had just completed a Fulbright scholarship in modern German and Austrian history at the University of Vienna in Austria, and now I faced my first real professional job in writing.

I remember going up the elevator at the old *Daily News* building at Madison Street and the Chicago River, finding my place on the society desk and looking out across the river at my beloved and magical hometown. I felt at that moment that anything was possible.

Yes, you already caught that, I was on the society desk. We had such journalistic creatures in those days, and I was working under the legendary, and quirky, society editor Athlyn Deshais, a little powerhouse of a woman who thought Chicago "society" was the most important thing in the paper. I'd like to be able to complain, but in fact that first job was a hell of a lot of fun.

But this was also the "moment" when journalism in the United States was changing for women; it didn't show yet, but it was happening. Indeed, that very first day on the job, the features editor, a big and charming Irishman named John Stanton, sent me out to interview a fan dancer. Soon after that, John asked me for some series ideas for the women's pages, as they were called then. I told him "abortion and interracial marriages," not exactly the staple of American newspaper ideas for nice ladies' pages in 1959. John said, "Fine." I did both, with no trouble at all.

A year later, I told the editors that I thought I should be on general assignment. Until then, there were only two women on general assignment, covering education and sob stories. I joined them. It was more fun than anyone should ever be able to have, covering the city and, soon, such national stories as the 1960 U.N. meeting when Fidel Castro (whom I would later interview many times and whose biography I would publish in 1991) visited New York and Nikita Khrushchev banged his frayed shoe on the table.

But what was probably my most noticed story came in 1963 when I masqueraded as a waitress at a big Mafia wedding at the Tam O'Shanter Country Club outside of Chicago. At these weddings, where a lot of business was done, the police and reporters were forced to wait out on the road while the sleaze of Mafia dons rode in in their black limousines. I never liked being kept out of anywhere, so I just marched in in my waitress uniform. When I left about three o'clock in the morning, the guards called me over. "Don't tell those reporters out there anything you saw," they instructed me. I assured them I would never do such a thing.

That's how it all began. In 1964, I went to Latin America and wrote for the paper. By 1967, I was covering Russia and Vietnam. By 1969, I added the Middle East, then Africa, Asia, and the whole world. It was a moment of opening for women and I was very lucky to be able to walk right into it. I always believed I belonged everywhere. In fact, I think we all do.

Here on a 1967 *Washington Week in Review* panel are Jack Nelson, *Los Angeles Times;* Harry Ellis, *Christian Science Monitor;* moderator Paul Duke; Georgie Anne Geyer, Los Angeles Times Syndicate; and Charles McDowell, *Richmond Times-Dispatch.*

Though thrilled to be in Mrs. Schiff's presence, the thrill was fleeting.

Phil Mushnick writes about the media for the *New York Post* and *TV Guide*.

In the fall of 1973, fresh out of college and drunk with ambition, I was hired by the *New York Post* as a lowly copyboy. The *Post,* at the time, was known as the liberal voice of New York City, and its elderly owner, Dorothy Schiff, was nationally celebrated as the champion of the poor and oppressed. In fact, the Mrs. Pynchon character on the *Lou Grant Show* was patterned after Mrs. Schiff, right down to the woman's overindulgence of her Yorkshire terrier.

I was at the newspaper perhaps three days when I was sent to the sixth floor. As I was making my way by elevator, the doors opened on the fourth floor and there stood Mrs. Schiff, as well as her chauffeur, whom I'd later learn was named Everitt.

"Lou Grant" (Ed Asner) visits the *Post* in 1979.

Everitt cradled the Yorkie.

Though thrilled to be in Mrs. Schiff's presence, the thrill was fleeting. Everitt motioned me out of the elevator. I looked at him as if I didn't understand. Well, I didn't. At that point he TOLD me to get out. Still not knowing exactly what he had in mind—did he want me to help him with some packages?—I obeyed. At that point, Mrs. Schiff, Everitt and Mrs. Schiff's mutt boarded the elevator and left me, humiliated and furious, standing in the fourth-floor hallway.

Upon returning to the city room, I told my story to a senior copyboy. He told me, without passion, that Mrs. Schiff doesn't share the elevator with employees other than Everitt, and that all employees are expected to surrender the elevator to her.

The next day's *Post* carried a short story about how Mrs. Schiff had, the night before, received her latest in a series of humanitarian awards. I've made my living as a cynic ever since.

I followed my instincts to the man whose name led the masthead.

My first newspaper job was a fluke and my career, most likely, a mistake—a statement I feel comfortable making without fear of violent dissension from some of my readers.

I had no formal journalism training, no qualifications, no connections—just a graduate degree in Spanish, a little pocket change and a lifelong affection for writing—when in June of 1977, I walked into the *Charleston (South Carolina) Evening Post*.

Even my going to Charleston was serendipitous, the result of a quick recitation of eeenie-meenie-mynie-moe at the intersection of I-95 and I-26. I was torn between stopovers in either Columbia or Charleston, both of which offered friendly cousins and clean sheets, so I took the logical, mature step of jabbing the air for directional inspiration. Moe apparently lives in Charleston and so, later that day, did I.

My first stop was in the publisher's office of the city's two family-owned newspapers. What did I know? This was the late 1970s before Lou Grant taught America how newsrooms work. Knowing nothing of newspaper hierarchy, I followed my instincts to the man whose name led the masthead. I figured he had to be the boss. Such were excellent instincts. Not only was he, Peter Manigault, the publisher, he was the owner. He also owned an English daily in Buenos Aires. After about an hour of chatting about our favorite Spanish poets, he hired me. Any literate person can be trained to be a reporter, he told me. Bless his heart.

You can imagine my warm welcome in the newsroom. Life immediately became miserable as the staff—this would be the J-school crowd—set out to teach me, if not the publisher, a lesson. I was sent to the hinterlands, commuting to distant bureau communities with names like Goose Creek and Monck's Corner. Now relatively chic bedroom communities of the city of steeples, in those days they were the sorts of places one might stop, for example, to pick up a jar of pickled pig's feet and a grape soda, or—say—how 'bout one of them Confederate flag bumper stickers!

My first "story," still curiously missing from compendiums of journalism's classic clutch-your-throat ledes, concerned a city council proposal to install

Kathleen Parker is a nationally syndicated columnist.

a left-turn signal at the town's single intersection. I've been no prouder of any byline since. Seeing my name, in bold type, centered above well-ordered paragraphs, well, you know how it is. I wanted nothing more than to spend the rest of my days amidst the loud cacophony of electric typewriters and printing presses and the doleful, glassy-eyed pleadings of hungover editors.

Those were the days, I'm old enough to say. Newsrooms were still noisy (and interesting). Ours was small, filled with metal desks, squeaky chairs, and fans. Beneath a large picture window, through which we could view actual weather, was an old shiny-worn leather couch upon which a certain lovely curmudgeon could be found napping most afternoons.

Some of the old guys had liquor bottles in their bottom drawers. Everybody smoked. Nary an Evian nor a disapproving glare in sight. Except from the copy desk toward me. Despite my immediate love affair with the newspaper business—and my earnest efforts to compose perfect sentences—copy editors nonetheless sneered at what they assumed was the publisher's pet when they corrected my humble profferings.

"It's our *style*," they'd hiss as they globbed through my sentences with a thick black marker. These were pre-computer days when editing was accomplished with various colored markers—black for delete and red for insert—and a scanner. Copy was always hard, composed on double-carboned paper.

I had no idea what "style" meant, and no one seemed interested in mentioning a spiral-bound blue book that would answer all my questions. Let her suffer, seemed to be the attitude, such that I usually went home in tears.

Then, one day my world changed. I managed through an accident of beginner's luck to get an unctuous city manager fired. That is to say, he lied and I caught him. Instant respect, instant liberation from copy editor glare. The story concerned tax millage, a subject about which I knew appropriately little. At $90 a week take-home pay, tax rates were of only slightly more compelling interest than initiation fees at the yacht club. But I was a reporter and asked the city manager to explain it to me.

> "Some of the old guys had liquor bottles in their bottom drawers. Everybody smoked. Nary an Evian nor a disapproving glare in sight."

In the course of paying attention, it dawned on me that the math didn't add up. This was an uncharacteristic act of genius for me, whose math skills are quantitatively nil; I probably should have been awarded a Nobel Prize. What I figured out was that the proposed millage increase was going to raise taxes ten times more than the amount he was telling citizens and city council members, who, I guess, didn't understand millage either. Anyway, once I wrote that he was fudging, he was fired.

And I was "promoted" . . . to sixteen-hour jobs in the city, covering all courts (city, county, state, and federal) and all city matters, producing no fewer than three stories before noon each day, the last one dictated over the phone from a courthouse. My editors' reasoning for this imponderable workload was exquisite. The buildings were across the street from each other.

In short, I was punished for wanting to write and rewarded for sticking it out, which sums up the essence of newspapering. Punishing and rewarding, rarely in equal doses. But I was hooked; I loved every excruciating minute of it; I relished every obit, the writing of which began each day for every reporter, regardless of tenure. I wept the day I left for another paper, another city.

Five newspapers and eight years later, I got a column for having a "voice," they told me. That was twelve years ago. I've written slightly fewer than a thousand columns. I hope to write a thousand more. I'm still working on "style."

I came to NBC News directly from print, no broadcast experience …

Ken Bode, a former NBC newsman, is the dean of the Medill School of Journalism at Northwestern University.

I came to NBC News directly from print, no broadcast experience whatsoever. Also, no voice coaches, no video coaches, no nothin'. "They throw you in," said my old friend Doug Kiker, "and if you stick, you stick."

With traditional television news stand-ups, the correspondent has a chance to try it three or four times until he/she gets it right. It's all on tape and it goes to the editing room where the producer selects the best effort and puts it in the spot. With live shots, there are no second chances.

Well, my first live shot came on the night of the 1980 New Hampshire primary, with me broadcasting from the NBC News Chicago bureau reporting a look-ahead at the upcoming primary in Wisconsin. I had a slight case of the rookie nerves. With a backdrop of Chicago's magnificent skyline behind me, I issued my analysis and handled all of Tom Brokaw's questions.

When it was over, I turned to my producer, Ted Elbert—soon to be the Moscow bureau chief for NBC News—and asked, "How'd I do, Ted?"

"Well, Bode," he replied, "to tell you the truth you looked a little stiff. But not so bad for a first time."

As promised, I went to the phone and called my parents, who'd watched my live network debut from their living room in Iowa. When my father answered, I asked him the same question: "How'd I do, Dad?"

"Well, son," he answered with his wonderful, blunt candor, "you looked like someone shoved a board up your ass."

I told that story as part of my father's eulogy.

... good things ... come in unforeseen, unpredictable ... ways.

It was shortly after World War II. My earliest, and only, ambition in life was to be either a play-by-play sports announcer or a sportswriter.

Upon my discharge from the Marine Corps at the Great Lakes Naval Station, I stayed over at nearby Evanston to find out if I might be accepted at Northwestern, then, as now, one of the country's best journalism schools. After being rejected, I returned home to Buffalo to attend the university there.

Late one night, unable to concentrate and floundering badly in my classes, I happened to pick up a copy of a magazine to pass the time. It was the October 25, 1947, issue of *Colliers*. The story that caught my attention was titled, "The Brain of the Bookies."

My love of sports, along with an occasional interest in betting, seemed an ideal match for this Minneapolis company, which set the odds on most of the major betting sports in the country. After reading this fascinating account of Leo Hirschfield, the publisher of Athletic Publications, I thought to myself, "Would I ever like to work for this man."

Without any encouragement or support from my family or friends for this wild-haired idea, I boarded a train to Minneapolis a couple of days later.

Leo hired me as a statistician. Two years later I was made one of the four handicappers responsible for setting the national odds, in addition to becoming the featured contributor to his major publication, the *Green Sheet*. Suffice to say, this experience opened the door to a life I never could have imagined. For the last forty-three years I have been absorbed, stimulated, challenged, thoroughly captivated and rewarded as the founder of the *Gold Sheet*.

And it all began because of a magazine article that triggered the pursuit of a dream I hadn't even known existed. It has been said that most of the good things that happen to us in life come in unforeseen, unpredictable, and circuitous ways. I can testify to this.

I sometimes wonder how the cards would have played had not that *Colliers* been there to lift me from a very low point in my life.

Mort Olshan is founder/editor of the *Gold Sheet*, a sports handicapping guide. He has written three books.

71

I was a man with a secret: ... I couldn't type.

Richard Reeves is a nationally syndicated columnist.

On an August day in 1963, I reported to the Morristown bureau of the old Newark, New Jersey, *Evening News.* I was a man with a secret: This was my first day at a daily newspaper and I couldn't type.

I came from a weekly newspaper I had started, the *Phillipsburg Free Press,* in the town where I worked as an engineer at Ingersoll-Rand. I was the editor. In fact, I was the whole editorial staff, working alone at night, after hours at I-R, on a Remington portable borrowed from my mother. Nobody ever saw me hunt and peck late at night. Now I was headed for the big time, I thought, and my wife and I took a week off, driving through New England. Each night, with a book called *How to Type,* I practiced hour after midnight hour, teaching myself to touch-type. I was up to twenty words a minute when I got to the *News.*

There were forest fires all over Jersey that day and I was sent to one in Sussex County. My job was to get a sidebar of some sort. I found a ranger who was on his last day of work after thirty years in the woods. Not bad.

But when I got back to the office, there was a stack of wire stories and files from other reporters around the state. "You're writing the lede," said my brand-new boss, the bureau chief, John W. Rae.

Scared out of my brain, I began my twenty wpm. "That's all you can do?" he said. "You're not going to make it here."

I immediately went back to my faster hunt-and-peck. I never learned to really type and I'm still mad at Johnny Rae, the bastard.

... Eyerly handed me five bucks and sent me ... to pick up his shirts.

I had a sensational summer in 1967 as an intern at the *Des Moines Register*. Or so I thought, until the last day.

Off and on throughout the entire summer, I worked on a story about a man in southeastern Iowa. He thought he might have found the skull of Pancho Villa, the Mexican bandit and revolutionary, in a trunk that had belonged to an obscure and long-deceased Iowa artist. Villa was assassinated in Mexico in 1923. Three years later, someone dug up his grave and hacked the skull from the corpse. It's never been found. For several reasons, my source in southeastern Iowa thought he might have fallen into possession of this grisly artifact.

My piece was going to be displayed prominently in the Sunday *Register* on the same day that I flew out of Des Moines to return to college. That Saturday night, my last at the newspaper, I straightened my tie and combed my hair on the way in to say good-bye to Frank Eyerly, the newspaper's legendarily gruff managing editor. I was expecting robust praise on my work that summer, congratulations on my Pancho Villa piece, and probably an open invitation to return to the *Register* after college. Instead, Eyerly handed me five bucks and sent me to a Chinese laundry to pick up his shirts.

That should have cured me. But the next morning, on the plane, I sat next to a stranger who'd carried the Sunday *Register* on board. I kept sneaking peeks as he got to my story about Pancho Villa's skull. He apparently read the whole piece, and with great interest. When he finished, I spoke up, asking what he thought of the story.

"Piece of bullshit," he said.

End of conversation.

And, very nearly, the end of my career in journalism.

John Carman is TV critic and columnist on the *San Francisco Chronicle*.

... the animal insisted on holding my hand.

Rita Braver is a reporter with CBS News.

Although I was hired to be a copygirl at WML-TV in New Orleans, I really wanted to write, report, and produce. Finally, my news director sent me out on assignment... to cover a chimpanzee as it made a visit to a hospital for sick children.

The visit went fine. The chimp entertained the kids and made them laugh. But on the way out, the animal insisted on holding my hand. Its handlers kept telling me this was fine, but suddenly the chimp let out a squeal and chomped down on my hand! Luckily, his teeth seemed to have been filed down, but the skin was broken and I was rushed off for a tetanus shot.

I ... worked hard at developing stories, rather than just "rip and read."

I had wanted to be in radio since the age of thirteen, when I bought a reel-to-reel recorder and practiced being a disc jockey. I studied speech in college and completed a Ph.D. in the same field. At twenty-seven, I became a professor of communications at Fitchburg, Massachusetts, State College. A guest speaker in my class one day was Mike O'Neil, program director at WEIM, the local radio station. We talked about my interest in radio and he offered me a weekend news job in December 1972. I loved the position and worked hard at developing stories, rather than just "rip and read."

One day in May of the next year, my new program director, Bob Cohen, came into the studio on a Saturday during my shift. He proceeded to tell me what an excellent job I was doing and that due to budget constraints my position was being eliminated. Ironically, we became close friends and, in fact, owned two radio stations together on an interim operator's license issued by the FCC. This is truly a strange business.

Mike Siegel is a nationally-syndicated talk show host.

... a career as a bartender wouldn't be such a bad thing.

Michael Knisley is a senior writer on the *Sporting News*.

I happened into my first job when an involuntary, compulsive spasm sent my arm into the air during an advanced reporting class in graduate school at the University of Colorado in 1975. The professor was handing out internships for the term. I listened, bored both with the available options and my chosen future career path. (I was of the opinion that those who can, do; those who can't, teach; and those who don't do either, write about it.)

Anyway, I didn't move a muscle as unappealing opportunities to cover the school board in Loveland and the city council in Longmont came and went. I was thinking that a career as a bartender wouldn't be such a bad thing. At the time, I was behind the bar part-time, an occupation that kept me wobbling over that fine line between getting the money to pay tuition and not getting the sleep to be in class often enough to make paying the tuition a sound investment. I was having a lot of fun at the bar, but that's another story.

Suddenly, before I could stop myself, I sensed myself raising my arm as the professor said these fateful words: "The *Boulder Daily Camera* needs someone to work the sports department." Next thing I knew, I was walking the sidelines, dodging acne-riddled, testosterone-laden teenagers in helmets and shoulder pads in the snow at a high school football so-called stadium (no press boxes at this level of the game), trying to keep statistics and play-by-play in a notebook soaked by snowflakes and my own runny nose.

Shortly after I filed that first soggy story, I went to my other job: tending bar. It was warm. It was dry. And every now and then, a pretty cocktail waitress smiled at me. Is it too late to go back behind the bar?

... the general manager invited me into the press box ...

I began as an unpaid intern for my hometown Rochester, New York, Red Wings, the Orioles' Triple-A affiliate. I was fifteen years old, and had been bringing my tape recorder to the games on my own, sitting in the stands, practicing my play-by-play while getting pelted with empty beer cups and half-eaten hot dog buns. One night, with about two hundred fans in the stands and temperatures around thirty-five degrees, one of the team's general managers took pity on me and invited me into the press box where they happened to have an empty booth. Nirvana! I went to work shmoozing instead of announcing and, before too long, had talked my way into an "internship," changing the carbonated Coke tank in the press box, running off copies of press releases, keeping track of the out-of-town scoreboard and glorious jobs like that.

The next summer, my role expanded to actually reading the scores on the Red Wings' radio broadcasts and, before too long, I was the full-time No. 2 announcer, for the princely sum of $20 per game.

I was still commuting to do my three innings a night all through college, and had gotten a raise up to $25 a night. For this fee, it was doing play-by-play plus writing and distributing the press notes, helping pull the tarp when it rained, answering phones, and, yes, still changing that !#%$ Coke tank. After graduation, the full-time No. 1 job opened up and for $1,000 a month, I was the voice of the Rochester Red Wings, a childhood dream come true.

It took five years of apprenticeship to get that gig, and another five before I graduated to the major leagues. Starting at fifteen was a tremendous advantage. By the time I was announcing big-league games at twenty-five, I felt like a seasoned veteran. The old ballpark in Rochester is gone now, but not my memories of sixteen-hour days and the chase for that gold ring of play-by-play on the radio. There is no greater job to have.

Josh Lewin is a baseball sportscaster for the Fox TV network. He also does play-by-play for the Detroit Tigers.

It has been 45 years, but the fear of exposure still haunts me.

Sam Lowe retired in 1999 as a columnist for the *Arizona Republic* in Phoenix.

It has been 45 years, but the fear of exposure still haunts me.

Someday, my personal nightmare goes, they'll find out that I don't really know how to write.

This stems from my first newspaper job, a position I acquired through a maneuver today's generation probably calls "truthful enhancement."

In 1955, I was a recently wed college dropout with no job and no job prospects. In desperation, I called the editor of my hometown newspaper, the Jamestown, North Dakota, *Sun*. I'd worked for them before. Twice. Once as a carrier; once as the kid who delivered papers to people who didn't get theirs.

In college, I had been the sports editor for the student newspaper, a job that consisted mainly of discussing the best places to find keg parties. These were probably not the best credentials, but I was broke, etc.

Bill Wright, the editor of the *Sun*, said the sports editor had quit that very day and they were looking for a replacement. He asked if I had experience. I didn't want to appear overqualified, so I didn't mention my days as a carrier. But the sports editorship got his attention, so he said, "Send me some clips."

After calling around to see what clips were, I hauled out my stack of college papers and started looking for my best stuff. There wasn't any. Not one thing I had written was worthy of inclusion on a job application. In near panic at the thought of losing a job I didn't even have, I cut my byline off a column, photocopied it several times and attached it to some presentable stories written by someone else. I wasn't like I was plagiarizing; it was only a job application. And, of course, I deserved some leniency because I was a newlywed.

Since copy machines weren't as sophisticated then as today, the forgeries looked pretty authentic. Especially after I used White-Out to get rid of those black lines around my alleged byline.

I took the train home and went to see Bill. He looked my stuff over, said it was fine, and then asked if I knew how to operate a camera. The past sports editor had also been the staff photographer. My knees were shaking and sweat was pouring from places I didn't even know I had, but it was too late to turn back. I assured him that my skills also included photography, so he handed me one of those old Speed Graphics, a twenty-five-pounder with a primary function of creating a clientele for hernia doctors.

There was a photo studio two blocks away. One of the owners was a friend. I ran there and unashamedly begged him to show me how to use the Graphic. He was a good friend. He removed the slide from the film holder, cocked the shutter and pointed me at a tree.

"Push the button," he said.

I did. He replaced the slide, took the holder into the dark room and processed the film. Within an hour, I was back at the newspaper office, photo in hand.

Bill was impressed and asked if I could start in two weeks. I said I'd be there. They ran my picture on the front page and said I was the new sports editor. My first assignment was a basketball game. It took four hours to write my report and the story was only three inches long, including box score, when it appeared the next day.

But it had my name on it.

And it was a legitimate byline.

So I had a job at $50 a week, and my mother was telling everyone in town how successful her son had become.

But things didn't go well at first. The deceit had to come out and it did, primarily because they didn't cover keg parties at the *Sun*.

Bill called me into his office.

"I know you never wrote those clips," he said. My hopes for a writing career hung in the balance.

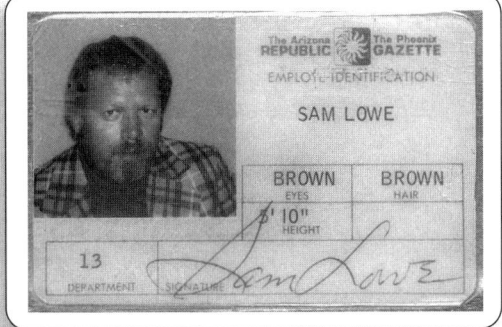

"But," he continued, "the boss likes you so you can stay on. Besides, we don't want to disappoint your mother."

I retired after a forty-five-year career as a managing editor, city editor, photographer and columnist. Maybe now I can stop worrying about my inability to write.

... It was remarkably small for a local and network news operation.

Marvin Kalb was chief diplomatic correspondent for CBS News and NBC News and moderator for *Meet the Press*. He is executive director of the Washington office of the Joan Shorenstein Center on the Press, Politics and Public Policy.

I had been hired by CBS News in June of 1957. I had just returned from a year or so in Moscow, where I had served as a translator and sometime press attaché at the U.S. embassy. I assumed, as I arrived on the seventeenth floor of 485 Madison Avenue in New York, the heart of CBS's vast global empire, that the newsroom would be abuzz with reporters and editors, shouting for attention and punching typewriters with urgent news.

But no. As I entered the newsroom at 11:45 P.M. for my midnight to 8 A.M. shift, I was struck by the fact that it was remarkably small for a local and network news operation—and strangely quiet. Four desks were crowded together, flanked on two sides by news wire machines, which click-clacked the news from around the world.

"You Marvin Kalb?" a portly editor asked, as he cleared his desk and prepared to leave. "You're responsible for the 5:30 A.M., the 6, the 6:30 and the 7. Scripts should be ready ten minutes before broadcast time." He then mumbled, "Oh, good luck," and he was gone. I was alone—me, totally inexperienced, untutored in the ways of professional journalism, and terrified.

I cleared a desk of old coffee cups and newspapers, and then, meticulously, as if each news item were a secret war report, I collected rolls of copy from The Associated Press, the United Press and Reuters, and arranged the stories in rows of copy, like troops at attention. I reread all the stories, searching for a possible lead for my 5:30 A.M. broadcast on WCBS, the local CBS radio affiliate.

By 2 A.M. or thereabouts, I became aware of an enveloping silence in the newsroom, as the tickers slowed to an occasional clack. At 3 A.M., I again checked the wires, wondering if anything was happening anywhere on this vast planet.

Bingo! There on Reuters was relatively short item from New Delhi. A boat carrying 327 people had capsized in the Ganges and, it was believed, no one had survived. I understood the news was terribly sad, but it was also fantastically liberating—I had my lead. "Bulletin from New Delhi!" I began writing, using the choppy radio lingo I had come to associate with the legendary Robert Trout. "An enormous tragedy hit India this morning," I continued. Etc. Etc. I timed my copy, reading it as I imagined Edward R. Murrow would have.

Shortly after 5 A.M., a cheerful man sporting a New York Yankees baseball cap entered the newsroom.

"Hello, Marvin Kalb." Hal Terkel pronounced in a voice much larger than, looking at him, I might have imagined. "Yes, sir," I said, happy that he knew my name, happier still that another human being had finally arrived to share my nocturnal anxiety. "Your 5:30 copy ready?" he asked. "Yes, sir," I repeated. "Right on your desk."

Terkel sat down, poured a cup of coffee, reached for the late edition of *New York Daily News* and opened it to the sports pages. 5:05 came and went. 5:10 came and went. When was he going to read my script? I wondered. At exactly 5:15, he put the *News* to one side, reached for a pencil, which I had sharpened, and began reading my script.

After a few minutes, he chirped, "Marvin, were there any Americans on that boat?" Christ! I muttered, and raced to my desk and reread the Reuters dispatch. "It doesn't say," I groaned. Terkel smiled. "The first thing we have to keep in mind," he said, "is that you're writing for local radio." He stressed the word "local." "The second thing is that it's the start of the July Fourth weekend. Right? Let's imagine you're a shopkeeper in Hempstead, Long Island, my home town." I kept sneaking a glance at the clock. We had a little more than twelve minutes to go before the 5:30 broadcast. "Now what would you want to know?" Terkel asked. "I'll tell you. You want to know what the weather's going to be like. You want to know who's pitching for the Yankees today against the Indians. You're sorry all those Indians died in the Ganges, but you're only interested in the Indians from Cleveland. Anyway, there are no Americans who died. So let's forget about the Ganges. You want to know what the mayor said about garbage collection and the strike in Brooklyn. And that's it."

Not waiting for any response from me, he quickly slipped a piece of copy paper in the Royal typewriter and, in less than nine minutes, completely rewrote my script and handed it to the announcer, who happened to saunter

> "'Now what would you want to know?' Terkel asked. 'I'll tell you. You want to know what the weather's going to be like. You want to know who's pitching for the Yankees today against the Indians.'"

past his desk on the way to Studio 17 with just a minute or two to go before the 5:30 broadcast.

It was my broadcast, but I didn't recognize it. It led with the weather, segued to the doubleheader at Yankee Stadium, which was to be attended by the mayor if the strike in Brooklyn did not distract him and the garbage collectors in Manhattan did not make more trouble. When the broadcast ended, Terkel asked if I had any questions before I started to write the 6 A.M. broadcast. "No, sir," I replied, "but can I call Reuters and ask if any Americans were on board?" Terkel said: "You can call, but I'm still not sure it's going to make the 6."

... the American cruiser USS Helena had been sunk ...

My first job was at WQXR radio (a classical music and hourly news station in New York City) in 1942 as night news editor, which meant I wrote the newscasts. Staff announcers read them on the air.

On the night in question, the Press Association ticker (PA was the radio arm of The Associated Press and WQXR's only ticker) rang its bulletin bell to alert all subscribers to an important bulletin. To my growing horror, it then printed out the news that the American cruiser *USS Helena* had been sunk by Japanese attack in the Kula Gulf. And the *Helena* was the ship on which my older brother was an officer. There was no further report on casualties or survivors.

I knew that our parents listened to every newscast I wrote for WQXR and would hear whatever I wrote. So for a few minutes, I agonized over whether to write the *Helena* sinking into my next newscast. That would grievously alarm our parents. But it didn't take more than that brief pause to recall my duty as a newsperson—to report the facts fully, fairly, and without personal alteration. I called home to warn my parents and I called the Navy public relations office for any word about survivors. They had no news. So without further details, the sinking of the *Helena* became the lead story of all the newscasts I wrote until the station signed off for the night.

My brother survived, with a Purple Heart, and was sent home for a brief rest, during which time he and I put on a program over WQXR, at the insistence of the Navy, recounting his adventure, and my reporting dilemma —all programmed to help sell war bonds. And, in fact, it sold quite a few bonds, mostly to family and friends.

But the whole affair brought home to me, long before I became a CBS News war correspondent in Korea, how deeply one's reports from the field can affect the families of people back home. In Korea, I wrote what I had to about casualties. That's genuine and important news. But I tried hard not to do any unnecessary reporting or frightening of listeners whose loved ones were in battle.

George Herman is a former reporter for CBS News.

"I'm going to wipe that grin off your face if it's the last thing I do."

P. S. Wall is a syndicated humor columnist with Universal Press Syndicate.

"If it bleeds, it leads!" the editor said, poking my forehead with his finger.

I wasn't sure if he was trying to hammer this bit of information through my thick skull or generate the next day's front-page headline, "Editor Lobotomizes Reporter with Fingernail."

On the long and winding road to finding myself, I got lost and ended up working as a newspaper reporter. My degree was in environmental science, so the cigar-eating editor stuck me chasing ambulances. Meanwhile, the environmental reporter couldn't pick a tree out of a police lineup. We called her Chicken Little because nobody could write a doomsday story like this chick. Not only did she have the readers convinced that the sky was falling and tap water would kill you, she once wrote a story about acid rain with the headline, "Air Being Polluted by LSD."

If Chicken Little made a mistake, Puckett gave her a slap on the wrist. If I screwed up, I got a tongue-lashing so bad the whites of my eyes got tobacco stains.

Puckett was of the school that the only good news was bad news.

"Fear sells papers," he said. "A reporter hasn't done his job unless the reader runs out and buys an attack dog, builds a bomb shelter and goes on antidepressants."

Needless to say, we had a teeny-tiny personality clash.

"Let me get this straight," Puckett said, flipping through my story. "You spend the whole day at a police station filled with hookers, murderers and thieves and you walk out with a story on 'America's Most Wanted Donuts.'"

"Believe it or not," I said, "it's your basic glazed."

"Are you a complete idiot?" he asked.

It's not that I didn't want to pump out yet another story about man's inhumanity to man, I just had a little trouble staying focused. Send me to cover a holdup, and I'd come back with a story about the immigrant family who arrived in this country with nothing but a falafel and now owns a chain of Minute Marts. Send me to a five-car pileup, and I'd write a story about the Edelweiss Club landscaping the Interstate median with poppies.

"Unless they're making opium out of those poppies to raise money for skinheads," Puckett yelled at me, "who cares?"

For Puckett, death, despair, and disease were not only inevitable—they were job security. And he made it his personal mission to bring me over to the dark side. Every hideous, hopeless, heartbreaking story that came along, Puckett sent me to crash the party.

"I'm going to wipe that grin off your face," he said, punctuating with his cigar, "if it's the last thing I do."

One day, I actually came back from covering a drug bust at the high school with a story about the drug bust. (The drug dog sniffed out half a joint in a student's car ashtray and twenty-seven bottles of Valium, Prozac, and Extra Strength Tylenol in the teachers' lounge.) Unfortunately, I also handed in a little sidepiece on the knockout Swedish foreign exchange student who was afraid of Jell-O.

"Olga calls Jell-O fruit-flavored fat," I said, standing in front of his desk. "When it jiggles, she passes out."

Opening his bottom drawer, Puckett pulled out a pint of Jack Daniels.

"Wall," he said, unscrewing the top for a little celebratory toast, "you're fired."

We stared at each other for a full thirty seconds.

"Was it something I said?" I grinned.

And that's how I became a humor columnist.

I had no way of knowing the full measure of my foolishness …

Jay Schadler is the creator, writer and hitchhiker for *TaleLights,* a new television series on the Bravo Network. He hosted ABC News specials entitled *Looking for America.*

My first job in television was as a weekday reporter and weekend anchor at WZZM-TV in Grand Rapids, Michigan. Now in television news, the weekends are largely populated by folks who are just beginning their broadcasting careers or rolling down toward the end. So the newsrooms and studios are brimming with passionate neophytes and bored veterans. Either way, it can be a recipe for on-air trouble. And so it was with me.

I was anchoring the weekend back in 1980. At the top of the eleven o'clock show, we would say "hello" and then tease our top three stories on a video screen behind the anchor. On this Saturday night, the headline stories and video (in order) were:

(1) Iraqi soldiers begin an offensive into Iran. Video—soldiers marching across desert.

(2) Grand Rapids City Council meets to discuss a school project. Video—council meeting.

(3) New Emporer penguins introduced into the local zoo. Video—tuxedoed birds sliding into water.

Naturally, I had written my anchor copy to accompany these stories and pictures. So far so good. But here comes the glitch. (Actually, at the time, it felt more like a career holocaust.). The director had inadvertently reversed the sequence of pictures, so when I said "Iraqi soldiers swept into Iran today," the video behind my shoulder showed sweet Emperor penguins sliding into their new pool at the zoo. And when I teased the penguin story, you guessed it, dusty troops were marching toward Tehran.

Of course, since all of this was being "chyroned" behind me, I had no way of knowing the full measure of my foolishness unfolding for our viewers. The barely muffled guffaws of the studio crew did, however, suggest my anchorman gravatis was somehow being severely compromised. Still, the delightful damage was done. And aside from the criminal charges filed against me for assaulting the director, I acquired an important value that's been my constant companion throughout the remainder of my career: humility.

"Young man," he said, "are you crazy?"

My first job after I was released from two undistinguished years of service in the Korean War was in the public relations department of the Southern Pacific railroad company in San Francisco. I had absolutely no interest in either public relations or trains, but since there were no newspaper jobs then available in the city for someone of my inexperience, and the pay at the S. P. was higher than I had any right to expect—a cool $395 a month—I became a railroad flack.

I loved living in San Francisco (still do), but hated the work, and when after three months of writing press releases I received a call from the *Berkeley Gazette* across the Bay saying a reporter's job had opened up, I instantly quit Southern Pacific and gratefully accepted employment that would pay me $100 less a month.

Before I left the railroad, though, I was called into the office of one of the company's senior vice presidents.

"Young man," he said, "are you crazy?"

I allowed as to how that was possible.

"How old are you?"

"Twenty-three."

"Well, don't you realize that almost everyone in your office here is past fifty and that the top two men, me included, are in their sixties and approaching retirement?"

I nodded.

"Don't you see that you could become a vice president of this company before you're thirty?"

I told him that a vice president of anything, including the United States of America, was exactly what I didn't want to become, that I wanted to write about something other than locomotives, and that at least since high school and certainly since college, all I'd ever wanted to be was a newspaperman.

The vice president regarded me with something approaching pity. And I'm certain he was thinking that someday this poor, irresponsible kid would actually grow up.

He was wrong about that.

Ron Fimrite has written for *Sports Illustrated* for thirty years.

... they had not hired me because of my portfolio ...

Bil Keane is the creator of "The Family Circus." Appearing in more than 1,500 newspapers, it is the most widely syndicated panel in America.

Before landing my first job in 1940 as an artist on the *Philadelphia Bulletin*, I put up with four years of a boring task every day after school. I had to deliver that same fat paper to eighty-five neighborhood customers. What a back-breaking chore! It was the pits! But I needed the money for art supplies.

Immediately upon graduation from high school, I compiled clippings of every cartoon and illustration I had done for the school magazine and for church publications. I added what, in my mind, was the most spectacular portfolio of original art since Norman Rockwell approached the *Saturday Evening Post*. I even had letters of recommendation from my uncle, who was a manager at Nabisco, and glowing character references from my father's political cohorts at Philadelphia City Hall. I then descended upon the personnel offices of the *Bulletin*, where I confidently filled out a detailed application.

Amazingly, I was hired! I was on my way to a cartoonist's career.

In a subsequent conversation with the *Bulletin*'s personnel manager, I found out that they had not hired me because of my portfolio, my pile of clippings, or my references. It was because I had done such an outstanding job of delivering the *Bulletin* daily to those eighty-five satisfied customers.

Bil at the *Philadelphia Bulletin* with some of the caricatures he drew for the entertainment section of the paper (late 1940s).

... you'd think he was firing you instead of editing your article.

Jonathan Alter is a columnist for *Newsweek* and a contributing correspondent for NBC News.

My first real job, after a few internships in journalism, was with the *Washington Monthly*, run by the legendary iconclast, Charlie Peters. Charlie runs a boot camp for young journalists—two or three at a time, for only two years or so each because the conditions are so bad. The pay: $8,400 a year (since raised to a princely $10,000). The hours: seventy to eighty a week. The responsibilities: Everything from writing cover stories to taking out the trash.

Charlie is famous for his "rain dance"—an editing session where he jumps up and down and yells and screams and tells you what's wrong with your piece and Washington and the state of the world and the way you were raised by your parents. It is simultaneously abusive and brilliant—the highest quality editing available anywhere in journalism, and also the wackiest. If you didn't know better, you'd think he was firing you instead of editing your article.

One day in 1982, Charlie had former Florida Governor Reubin Askew in to talk; Askew was then thinking of running for president in 1984 (he decided not to). Askew's interview with Charlie lasted about as long as my job interview—five minutes, max. (Charlie makes up his mind about people fast). We felt a little bad about hauling Askew up to our humble townhouse in the low-rent Adams-Morgan neighborhood of Washington, D.C., so my colleague and I continued the conversation outside Charlie's closed door. The exterminator had just been in, so the place reeked. And the roaches were being blasted out of the walls.

My most distinct memory of that day was simultaneously seeing a roach heading off the banister and onto Governor Askew's head as the intercom in my office buzzed over and over. I had to decide: roach or intercom? I finally grabbed the insistent intercom and it was Charlie:

"Is he gone yet?"

"No, we're still talking to him, why?" I said.

"Because I have to go to the bathroom. I've already said my good-byes to the Governor and I don't want to say them again. Get him out of there."

And we did, leaving the roaches to find new prey.

... I did not have to support myself, but depended on my father ...

My introduction to journalism was far removed from that of the customary aspiring journalist. In fact, I did not intend or even aspire to become a writer of any kind. That was because of my instructor in freshman English at Smith College. He was not the regular teacher, who presumably did what so many college professors of today do—enlist the services of an advanced student so the professor can devote his time to writing a book. In any case, by the end of that year I was so alienated from compositions of any kind that I avoided writing courses for my remaining three years. So how on Earth did I end up in a writing career?

It began with a telephone call from the then-society editor of the *Washington Post*, Hope Ridings Miller, asking if I would write a weekly column for the *Post*. I had sought her out previously to get publicity for a Washington Junior League fundraising project, and she apparently thought my release indicated I could write well enough for her purposes. Her main reason was my familiarity with the social scene in Washington, where I had lived all my life.

I remember being reluctant to accept her offer. How did she know I would meet my deadlines? I asked. She said she wasn't worried about that. So I, thinking it might lead to some other job I would love, said OK and took over the Sunday column already entitled "Top Hats and Tiaras." We didn't mess around with egalitarianism in those days. People who had money weren't considered villains.

After having fun with that column for three years, my health, which had never been robust, deteriorated. The prognosis at the Mayo Clinic was simply that my ambition exceeded my strength and I should get ten or eleven hours of sleep every night for two years! Obviously, covering parties under that dictum was impossible, so I resigned. With no improvement after two years, I took up Christian Science and in four months I was much better.

Eager to get back to work, I went to see managing editor Herbert Corn of the *Evening Star*, then the leading newspaper in Washington and one of the most successful in the country. I took with me the sketch I had written about an outstanding Washingtonian

Betty Beale wrote a society column for the *Washington Post* and, later, the *Washington Star*. She wrote a weekly syndicated column for more than thirty-five years. Her autobiography is entitled, *Power at Play: A Memoir of Parties, Politicians and Presidents in My Bedroom*.

> "The entire staff was put to work on the presidential parties by calling the ranking women attending to ask if they were wearing cerise taffeta, purple velvet, black crepe or whatever. Such gripping information was woven into the completed story before the affair was held."

revealing his identity only in the last line, a format I hoped to sell as a weekly feature. Instead, Mr. Corn offered me a job in the *Star*'s society department. I took it and quickly found out that the four or five other women in the department spent most of their time writing up weddings based on the facts dropped on their desks daily by girls from all walks of life—most of them far removed from the known social strata. When I complained about all those veiled unknown brides in the paper, the society editor's incredible reply was, "What would we put in the paper then?" "News," I replied, a comment not appreciated.

The Sunday *Star* sometimes carried from four to six pages of those veiled faces—forty-eight brides to a page—because editor-in-chief Benjamin McKelway thought they were "friendship builders," even though at least half didn't subscribe to the *Star*.

The two oldest women in the department had been there for years, starting at $5 a week. The Newspaper Guild had moved in a few years before I joined them and, if I recall correctly, my starting salary was about $49 a week. Fortunately, I did not have to support myself, but depended on my father, who was vice president of a bank.

Naturally, hostesses who wanted their parties in the paper sent invitations to each newspaper society editor, and in those days the White House sent an invitation to the traditional five official dinners and five official receptions held annually. The entire staff was put to work on the presidential parties by calling the ranking women attending to ask if they were wearing cerise taffeta, purple velvet, black crepe or whatever. Such gripping information was woven into the completed story before the affair was held. The reporter covering it only had to check the galley after the event to see what, if anything, needed to be changed.

As I had invitations on my own, I began writing up the cocktail and dinner parties I went to almost nightly in a weekly Sunday column which I called "Exclusively Yours," and which gradually turned into four a week. And soon I was receiving White House invitations. From Harry Truman's administration through Ronald Reagan's, I covered the glamorous doings of eight presidents—in the *Star* until it folded in August of 1981, and in the syndicated column that I wrote from 1953 until 1989. During that time I met and spoke to kings, queens, presidents and prime ministers from around the world, as well as the heads in our own government, foreign ambassadors and scads of American celebrities who began being invited to the White House during the Kennedy administration.

My favorite king was Juan Carlos of Spain, who began coming to Washington when he was a prince and who, by the time he became king, seemed to regard me as an old friend, because he kissed me on the cheek when I went through the embassy reception line. And more impressive than that, he leaned over and kissed my hand at the big reception he and Queen Sophia gave at the Corcoran Art Gallery during one visit. To have a reigning king kiss one's hand—the opposite of the action one associates with kings—gave me a thrill, I have to admit. But it quickly turned into aggravation when I discovered that not a single photographer in the crowd of cameramen surrounding us, including the one I took with me, snapped that picture!

So the phone call had led to something interesting after all.

At the back of the room, an old press thundered randomly.

Ben Beagle was a columnist for the *Roanoke (Virginia) Times* for forty-one years.

In the fall of 1953, I reported to the *Staunton (Virginia) News-Leader*—the publisher of which was a retired National Guard general. The pay was $55 for a six-day week and six cents for mileage in my 1950 Ford with ninety thousand miles on it and a defective heater in it.

The newsroom was up a dusty staircase—a tiny, foreboding place in which I would work as the nightside reporter on a morning daily. The only other human in the room was the city editor, who liked to drink and cover the school board. Downstairs were the business offices and composing room—the former staffed mainly by the general's female relatives and the latter by deaf mutes from the nearby Virginia School for the Deaf and Blind. They were the best composing room people I ever knew.

At the back of the room, an old press thundered randomly. I don't know what kind it was, but I do know that the nightside press foreman, a skillful drunk named Dick, used to crawl all over the thing when it was running. And there were bets about whether he would fall in sometime and become, perhaps, part of the society page.

The general was a thrifty sort. The copy paper we used was the back of teletype paper that hadn't been sent down the chute for printing. You used old newsprint fragments for your notes when on assignment, or you got fancy and bought your own spiral notebook—a major expenditure when you were making $55 a week.

The city editor taught me a lot of the fundamentals of the newspaper trade and I still admire him—and even admire his drinking habits. He was an intellectual, trapped in a small room on Central Avenue in Staunton, Virginia, and he enjoyed it. Every time he started quoting "The Wreck of the Hesperus," you knew he had a bottle of Old Grand Dad hidden in the general's desk downstairs. And he would use this bottle all night.

My finest hour in the print business may have come on the Saturday night he got drunk and started dancing around the composing room, throwing rolls of that used Associated Press copy paper around like party streamers. I had to compose the front page—a thing I had never done before—and in those days when non-union papers let interlopers like me touch the type, I did the best I could. The head compositor —a very smart person from Virginia's Rockbridge Baths—made the following comment:

"You done good, Ben. Now the only thing we need is a box that'll tell people how to read the front page."

... a small story now might rescue him from a big story later.

Tom Tiede has been a syndicated national, foreign, and war correspondent, a newspaper publisher, and a newspaper owner.

When I graduated from college, and *The New York Times* laughed at my job applications, I started work as a sports editor for the *Kalispell Daily InterLake.* Kalispell is in Montana, where little is easy. Thus, in addition to my regular duties—reporting the wonders of Babe Ruth League baseball—I wrote what used to be called the crime blurbs from what used to be called the police blotter.

You know: "An officer arrested a man for drunken driving yesterday after watching him drive around and around a downtown block. The officer said the man told him that his turn blinker was stuck."

It was not the stuff of Pulitzer prizes, but there were some moments. One day, the police reported that one of the town's leading merchants and citizens had been charged with exposing himself in public, which used to be called flashing. I wrote the usual four paragraphs, each of which was promptly killed by the publisher. (Uh, it used to be called "spiked.")

The publisher, Joe Caraher, said there were extenuating circumstances in the matter. He said the perp was drunk, for one thing, and, for another, he was the newspaper's biggest advertiser. Joe said the man had begged him not to run a story that would ruin his life and destroy his family.

I argued that it was not journalism's place to weigh results. I argued, too, that there would be no question about reporting the antics of someone with less muscle. I also fell back on the philosophy that, if the guy did have problems of this kind, a small story now might rescue him from a big story later.

Guess who won the day?

I left Kalispell soon after, ripe with indignation, vowing ever to be cold of heart and fearless in this business.

Many years later, I owned a newspaper of my own, in Bryan County, Georgia. I learned there that one of the municipal judges had served time in federal prison for participating in a narcotics theft. The judge said he was drunk at the time and begged me not to run a story that would ruin his life and destroy his family. He likewise said his mother was ill, and this might kill her.

Guess who won that day?

And he didn't even advertise.

The only absolute truth I've gathered in journalism, as in life, is that everything is in reference to choices. Sometimes you make the right ones, sometimes the wrong ones, and it's well not to keep close score.

"The only absolute truth I've gathered in journalism, as in life, is that everything is in reference to choices."

My first investigative work was an exposé on our mayor ...

Bob Hill is a metro columnist on the *Louisville (Kentucky) Courier-Journal*.

What I most remember about my first newspaper job was the Saturday mornings. I had become editor of biweekly papers in Sycamore, Illinois, mostly by default. I had no journalism experience, had never taken a college journalism course, and wrote everything in ragged longhand, usually with a pencil.

I had just quit an entry-level job with the Chrysler Corporation in which I sat in a football field-sized room with about 250 other men ordering parts from people we never saw to build a car I couldn't afford to drive. Fed up, drinking too much, and convinced I wanted to be a writer, I quit the car business and applied for a job as editor of the *Sycamore Sun Tribune* and *True Republican*.

I had two things going for me. One, Sycamore was my hometown. Two, nobody else applied for a job that paid $105 a week, provided no benefits, and offered a solid opportunity to work sixty hours a week. I couldn't wait to get at it.

Writing, as I now tell any high school or college student who will listen, finds you. It can't be ignored. It won't go away. If I wasn't hooked going in, my career path was set in granite the day my first column appeared in print: silly, sophomoric, imitative, but mine.

I worked behind a large, wooden, and badly-scarred desk with a view of Main Street. My first investigative work was an exposé on our mayor, who worked in a furniture store across the street and too often parked in a no-parking zone. We ran a photo of his car in the offending slot. The mayor—twenty-five years in office—was appalled. Woodward and Bernstein should have been so lucky.

I also learned the value of situational ethics. Our local VFW, a favorite watering hole, earned the bulk of its income through illegal slot machines. We let that one go in the interest of honoring war veterans.

The logo on the side of our delivery van, cheap and pale white, said, "Weekly But Strongly." Our red brick building was a museum. There was an old Linotype machine in the basement, stacks of old papers in dark corners, pieces of lead type on the floor. Years later the bank bought it and built a drive-through window next to it.

My favorite journalistic moments came every Saturday morning. I went into the office alone. The editor was at his desk, going through a six-inch stack of mailed press releases from various agricultural interests, political hacks and arts groups in search of a single paragraph of help and moral support.

I'd sit there, feeling equally lost and worthwhile, mulling over future columns, ideas for features, dreaming up ways to build circulation, and trying to get people I'd grown up with to understand this was really something I wanted to do. Every once in a while, I'd peek out the window to see if the mayor was in the furniture store.

> "I also learned the value of situational ethics. Our local VFW, a favorite watering hole, earned the bulk of its income through illegal slot machines. We let that one go in the interest of honoring war veterans."

It still hadn't sunk into my head that he was offering me a job.

For more than twenty years, **Paul Harris** has hosted radio shows in Washington, D.C., New York City, Hartford, Connecticut, and Philadelphia. He has a midday talk show on KTRS in St. Louis.

My first interview at radio station WRCN in Riverhead, New York, was on Monday, April 3, 1978, a beautiful spring Long Island day.

I pulled into the driveway off Flanders Road into the abandoned Riverhead Drive-In. One hundred yards up on the right was a one-story cinderblock building, which I had been told was the radio station studios. Outside in the small gravel parking lot I saw two guys throwing a softball. I learned later that one of them was Charlie, the chief engineer, and the other was Jeff Fisher, the music director and midday jock, who also happened to be on the air at the time. They greeted me and said that Don Brink, the program director, was in his office, just outside the door and to the left. As I walked in, Jeff ran back in to segue into the next record on the air. Then he was back out in the parking lot to resume that game of catch.

Don, the morning man as well as program director, sat me down in his small office and began to talk with me about radio in general and WRCN's format in particular. He handed me a looseleaf notebook containing the formatic basics. It still hadn't sunk into my head that he was offering me a job. All of a sudden he said, "I can't get you on by this weekend, so how about if your first night is Saturday the fifteenth?" I stammered out something like, "Sure, that sounds good." He smiled and then introduced me to the rest of the crew.

He showed me the furnace room, also the home of the UPI newswire that was constantly spitting out rolls of yellow paper with the latest news, sports and weather stories. Down the hall was the transmitter—a huge piece of equipment that gave off so much heat the DJs used the tubes to keep hamburgers warm. Then, into the studio, which was so tiny it could hold only two people at a time. I watched Jeff do a couple of segues and then talk on the air. Although I had been on the air and behind microphones for several years already, I was nervous being in there. I swallowed hard, realizing that I'd be sitting in that seat in less than two weeks.

Soon Don returned and showed me the production studio, the music director's office, and the engineer's area, which was nothing more than a workbench full of equipment. Then he walked me back to the front door—a distance of twenty feet—and out to my car. He told me to come in about an hour early on the fifteenth to watch the previous jock do the last hour of his show and then I'd be on from 7 P.M. to midnight. I agreed and thanked him for the opportunity.

On the way home, and for the next week and a half, I spent every spare moment listening closely to WRCN, trying to pick out the different elements of the format. In just twelve days, I would make my debut on commercial radio!

... increasingly difficult to come up with passable cartoon ideas.

Jim Berry pens his widely-syndicated "Berry's World" for Newspaper Enterprise Association. He is a five-time winner of National Cartoonists Society awards.

For several years, when I was in my late twenties, my dream was to create a successful syndicated comic strip. After serving in the Navy, working in the field of animation, being in the retail automobile business, and then joining a consulting firm, I was hired to work at the Newspaper Enterprise Association headquarters in Cleveland, Ohio, in 1961. It was my first job in the print media.

I worked in the editorial department. My job was doing everything from creating little "goomie" filler drawings to hand-lettering the answers to crossword puzzles. Fortunately, I was given an opportunity to do some regular editorial cartoons for the NEA

service. My work was carefully checked by an editor who was also the big boss. Within six months, one of my cartoons was published in the "Week in Review" section of the Sunday *New York Times*. What a thrill. My wife Heather and I went out for dinner and toasted to this recognition with champagne. I was hooked on editorial cartooning.

On a different note, one of my duties was to create innocuous editorial cartoons for the NEA service for weekly newspapers. These efforts were edited by a fellow who had more ideas about why a cartoon could not be done than I could imagine possible. For example, one of the many "don'ts" was never to show people watching television. Television was the rival of our client newspapers and he felt we should not promote TV. Another "don't" was never to draw people inside a discount-type store. Department stores buy ads in newspapers, I was told, and they did not want to see their competition given publicity. These "don'ts" seemed endless. To me, it was stultifying. Over time, it became increasingly difficult to come up with passable cartoon ideas. There were times that I was ready to throw in the towel. If I had had to work with that particular editor much longer, I think I probably would have given up. Come to think of it, I came close to not becoming a professional cartoonist because of him.

After about a year of being directed by that hidebound editor, "Berry's World" was launched, and it was bye-bye weekly columns and bye-bye rules man. I was moved out of the Editorial Art Department to the Comic Art Department.

> "For example, one of the many 'don'ts' was never to show people watching television. Television was the rival of our client newspapers and he felt we should not promote TV."

Of course ... it wound up costing me fifty bucks a game.

Steve Levy is a sportscaster on ESPN.

I was lucky enough to land my first professional job while still in college. And it wasn't on just any station. It was the flame-throwing, 50,000-watt WABC Radio in New York City. It was a kick because that's where I grew up, so my folks and friends could listen to me. I was a stringer. During my sophomore year at the State University of New York at Oswego, I was assigned to all Buffalo Bills home games. Three reports per game, one pre-game which I taped over the phone from my dorm room on Friday afternoon, and then halftime and post-game from the stadium—each sixty seconds in length. I was paid $50 per game. Of course by the time I was through, it wound up costing me fifty bucks a game. I had to rent a car and pay gas and tolls. Keep in mind that I was a college student. After a typical Saturday night, I had to leave at around 8 A.M. to make the three-hour drive to Buffalo.

One morning, after a particularly difficult Saturday night, I was running late. I was never going to make it to the stadium by halftime, so I drove as fast as I could and as far as I could, listening to the game on the radio and taking the best notes I could. I phoned in my halftime report live from a Burger King at one of the truck stops off the New York Turnpike. I got a lot of interesting looks from folks ordering Whoppers when I said "Live from Rich Stadium" instead of "Live from Burger King."

I chose a course in journalism rather than in the food industry.

In 1981, I was sprung from the University of Florida's venerable School of Communications and Journalism. Eager to inflict my skills on the Republic, I accepted a $180-a-week position at a small radio station in Sarasota, Florida. While the local Benigan's offered more money, I chose a course in journalism rather than in the food industry. I was young and foolish.

To this day, I still ache with nostalgia when I recall Sundays at WQSA-AM. Between playing inaudible, hour-long church tapes, I honed my journalism craft by scraping dead mouse chunks off the counter behind the station's yeoman coffee-maker.

I still get misty-eyed remembering one early morning when I spread the news to our sixteen listeners before realizing I had never turned the radio station on. That darn transmitter! Oh, the laughs we had over my goof! Soon after that, I accepted a position in Orlando, where there were many more Benigan's.

By the way, the station owner, a Mr. Ted Rodgers, was a public relations or consultant guy at the Nixon-Kennedy debate. Occasionally, I see old news programs about the famous debate and there's my old boss being interviewed.

But I knew him when—when I forgot to turn on his radio station.

Rob Hiaasen writes for the *Baltimore Sun*. His stories have appeared in more than fifty newspapers. In 1992 he was nominated for the Pulitzer Prize.

I was sent to interview a couple who practiced witchcraft.

Barbara Naness penned the nationally syndicated column, "In a Nutshell."

While working as a reporter for the *Staten Island Register*, I was assigned a Halloween story. I was sent to interview a couple who practiced witchcraft.

True to their non-traditional lifestyle, they lived in a run-down walk-up apartment in a decrepit old building. How eerily appropriate, I thought as I climbed the rickety stairs. The place really gave me the creeps.

The apartment was dimly lit and cluttered with pagan paraphernalia. We sat on chairs in the living room and, after taking out my notebook and pen, I absentmindedly placed my pocketbook on the floor next to me.

For the next hour or so, the pair fascinated me with stories about their rituals, spells and icons. I just knew this was going to be one of my more memorable assignments.

It was only after I arrived home that night that I learned one of the most basic and integral rules of journalism: Never put your pocketbook on the floor. As I placed my bag on the kitchen counter and opened it to take out my notebook, out crawled a great big roach.

It was memorable, all right.

I was ... planning on going out and changing the world.

Six months after I was hired as the sports staff of a small-circulation afternoon daily in Central California, the managing editor took me to lunch.

I can't remember all that he said—most words spoken by editors don't stick anyhow—but I remember something about my having done a decent job with page design and covering high school sports. I had been a stringer for the *Daily Report,* my hometown newspaper in Southern California, for two years in high school and parts of summers while home from college. But I hadn't planned on being a journalist. It was the mid-'60s. I was a sociology major, planning on going out and changing the world. It didn't quite happen that way.

A few months after my college graduation the sports editor of my hometown paper, apparently having sympathy for someone willing to work for low wages in order to "change the world," told me about a job a few hours north. Full-time. Probably split shifts and six-day work weeks. Some benefits. All of $85 a week. Why not? It was in the grape strike area, and at least I'd get to do some stories.

But it didn't happen. Sports isn't grapes, I learned. And grapes weren't even news to most papers. So I did sports, with some occasional news of meetings and routine items. For two weeks while the society editor was on vacation, the managing editor and I did engagements, weddings, PTA meetings —and sports.

At some point, I figured out that a lot of sports weren't being covered, just as all the news wasn't being covered. I couldn't do everything, and there was no money for stringers. The best I could do was to take calls from coaches, go into the field every now and then, add the wire copy, dummy the page or two, and send them on to press, hopefully by deadline. But there never was enough room for what needed to be covered.

Advertising was decent, but the newshole wasn't. Every day, interesting stories were dumped because the sports pages began looking more like ad pages.

Being young, naïve, and an activist at heart, I protested. But it was a lame protest since I was told that advertising was important. I complained again. Just fill space, I was told. Try to find "the most important" stories.

Walt Brasch worked on three newspapers and is now a university professor of journalism specializing in social issues.

"It's easy to sacrifice news; the one thing you can't sacrifice is advertising."

One day, I had a lot of solid news and sports to dummy, but very little space. That's not the way it's supposed to be, I figured. I don't remember whether any of the other six editorial staff members ever thought that way, but I know I did. News is supposed to be important. I also don't remember if I was frustrated or just trying to be funny, but at the top of the dummy page, I crossed out "Sports" and handwrote "Ad Page."

And now I was sitting in some restaurant near the newspaper. And the managing editor was telling me I was getting better, that my writing and reporting were good—with a few problems here and there—that the page makeup was decent—and that it "just isn't working out." He was sorry. He was such a nice guy that I felt sorry for him having to tell me this.

A few weeks later, in mid-America, I was a general assignment reporter for another organization. Nice people, both on the staff and in the community. Much better pay, but still relatively low compared to what other college graduates were making. Minimal benefits. Long work week. No union, obviously. But I never forgot a lesson from my first full-time job. It's easy to sacrifice news; the one thing you can't sacrifice is advertising.

Index

Alter, Jonathan, *Newsweek,* NBC News, 90

Amanpour, Christiane, CNN, 4

Bayé, Betty Winston, *Louisville Courier-Journal,* 59

Beagle, Ben, *Roanoke (Virginia) Times,* 94

Beale, Betty, *Washington Post, Washington Star,* 91

Becka, Tom, KFAB, Omaha, 21

Berry, Jim, nationally syndicated cartoonist, 102

Bode, Ken, Medill School of Journalism, Northwestern University, 70

Boyle, Mark, Indianapolis Pacers, 12

Brasch, Walt, professor of journalism, 107

Braver, Rita, CBS News, 74

Bykofsky, Stu, *Philadelphia Daily News,* 32

Carman, John, *San Francisco Chronicle,* 73

Carry, B. Peter, *Sports Illustrated,* 46

Cushman, Tom, *San Diego Union-Tribune,* 25

Dancy, John, NBC News, 11

Fimrite, Ron, *Sports Illustrated,* 87

Forbes, Gordon, *USA Today,* 42

Geyer, Georgie Anne, nationally syndicated columnist, 64

Halberstam, David, Miami Heat, 24

Harlan, Kevin, CBS Sports, Turner Sports, 54

Harris, Paul, KTRS St. Louis, 100

Herman, George, CBS News, 83

Hiaasen, Rob, *Baltimore Sun,* 107

Hill, Bob, *Louisville Courier-Journal,* 98

Hughes, Pat, WGN Chicago, 16

Johnson, Ernie, Milwaukee Braves, 43

Johnson, Rheta Grimsley, *Atlanta Constitution* & King Features Syndicate, 17

Kalb, Marvin, Joan Shorenstein Center on the Press, Politics and Public Policy, 80

Keane, Bil, nationally syndicated cartoonist, 88

Knisley, Michael, *Sporting News,* 76

Lardner, George, *Washington Post,* 63

Lawrence, Jill, *USA Today,* 5

Levy, Steve, ESPN, 104

Lewin, Josh, Fox TV, 77

Linkletter, Art, television personality, 3

Litke, Jim, The Associated Press, 18

Lowe, Sam, *Arizona Republic,* 78

Mathews, Garret, *Evansville (Indiana) Courier & Press,* x

Mayne, Kenny, ESPN, 35

McCaslin, John, *Washington (D.C.) Times*, 14

McCoy, Hal, *Dayton Daily News*, 44

Mears, Walter, Associated Press, 7

Morton, Bruce, CNN, 48

Mushnick, Phil, *New York Post, TV Guide*, 66

Naness, Barbara, nationally syndicated columnist, 106

Olderman, Murray, *Palm Springs (California) Life*, 26

Olshan, Mort, *Gold Sheet*, 71

Parker, Kathleen, nationally syndicated columnist, 67

Perkins, Jack, Arts & Entertainment Network, 56

Reeves, Richard, nationally syndicated columnist, 72

Roan, Dan, WGN-TV Chicago, 20

Robarchek, Doug, *Charlotte (North Carolina) Observer*, 36

Schadler, Jay, Bravo Network, 86

Shaw, David, *Los Angeles Times*, 49

Siegel, Mike, nationally syndicated talk show host, 75

Simon, Roger, *U.S. News & World Report*, 52

Storin, Matthew, *Boston Globe*, 6

Stratton, Gil, CBS, 51

Tait, Joe, Cleveland Cavaliers, 31

Tammeus, Bill, *Kansas City Star*, 22

Thiel, Art, *Seattle Post-Intelligencer*, 50

Tiede, Tom, nationally syndicated correspondent, 96

Vecsey, George, *The New York Times*, 38

Verdi, Bob, *Golf Digest*, 10

Viets, Elaine, nationally syndicated columnist, 60

Vincent, Charlie, *Detroit Free Press*, 28

Walker, Mort, nationally syndicated cartoonist, 8

Wall, P. S., Universal Press Syndicate, ix, 84

Williams, Juan, *Washington Post*, 55

Wolff, Alexander, *Sports Illustrated*, 13

Zumoff, Marc, Philadelphia '76ers, 58